THE THREE MARKS
OF MANHOOD

*How to Be Priest, Prophet,
and King of Your Family*

G. C. Dilsaver

TAN Books
Charlotte, North Carolina

ISBN: 978-0-89555-904-3

Cover design by Tony Pro.
Cover image: Sistine Chapel Ceiling (1508-12): *The Creation of Adam*, 1511-12 (fresco) (post restoration) by Michelangelo Buonarroti (1475-1564). Vatican Museums and Galleries, Vatican City, Italy/The Bridgeman Art Library.

Printed and bound in the United States of America.

TAN Books
Charlotte, North Carolina
2010

THE THREE MARKS
OF MANHOOD

CONTENTS

INTRODUCTION

THE CHRISTIAN FAMILY is a patriarchal hierarchy. So teaches the Catholic Church in Scripture, in the Roman Catechism, and in modern encyclicals. As a patriarchal hierarchy it reflects the hierarchy of the Church; it also reflects the hierarchy of divine government itself, which is manifest not only in God's rule over His creation, but in the relationships of the Trinity, whose absolute unity derives from the subordination of the Son to the Father.

Why, then, is this teaching such a hard saying for modern ears? Even among orthodox Catholics, the mention of Christian patriarchy is liable to elicit some negative reaction. To begin with, the very term "patriarchy" has been turned into a pejorative by today's manipulators of language and enforcers of political correctness. Contemporary liberal society's espousal of the ideology hyper-egalitarianism saturates every facet of the secular realm. With this ideology promulgated by the schools, the mass media, the corporations, and the state, it is in the very air we breathe. One cannot help but be swayed by such an all pervasive propagandizing.

And it is modern feminism that is hyper-egalitarianism's banner issue. Used by the state as fulcrum against the unacceptable non-governmental authority of the family, it is a powerful and pernicious movement indeed. For what other movement has won the right, the societal approbation, to murder at will? A feminist disposition, its spirit and politics, has become an essential requirement for those who seek to function in secular society. And feminism's greatest foe, its very antithesis, is patriarchy.

The hard saying of patriarchy is more painful still in that it

touches on the specific sore spot of our time: the dissolution
of the traditional family. It is characteristic of lay Catholics of
a traditional or conservative bent to be ever in search of an
explanatory analysis of what went wrong with society and the
Church. Most of the explanations they find, valid as they may
be, are in areas out of their influence or competency, such as
liturgical or ecclesiological issues. Hence it is also characteristic
of such Catholics to feel a deep frustration. But there is one
area that the laity have full competency to reform and make as
Catholic as they wish, and this area is the key to all the other
besetting problems. It is the family. Order the home and the
rest will follow. And the perennial—and definitively Catholic—
order of the home is that of patriarchy.

Wives are to be submissive and obedient to their husbands,
loving and honoring them second only to God alone. Husbands
are to be uniquely devoted to their wives, loving them more than
their very selves and giving their lives for them as Christ did for
the Church. These tasks are difficult, but achievable with God's
grace, which is made available through Holy Matrimony and
the other sacraments.

As His Holiness Pope John Paul II often pointed out,[1] there
have been abuses of the "male prerogative" that have remained
even in Christian cultures. This is not surprising, since such
abuses are part and parcel of fallen, sinful human nature. To
the degree that such abuses prevail, a true Christian patriarchy is not present. For although a sinful act often superficially
resembles a virtuous one (for instance, an illicit sexual act and
the marital act), that resemblance does not redound on the virtuous act. In the same manner, the presence of worldly structures of brute and self-seeking domination should not sully,
but should rather contrastingly accent, the honor and splendor

---

1. See Appendix A

of a Christian patriarchy characterized by loving service and sacrificial leadership.

Note well that the call to Christian patriarchy is a call to service and love rather than selfishness and arrogance, thus it is a call that in more ways than one is contrary to modern sensibilities. The authentic Christian patriarch must constantly die to himself, that is, constantly do violence to his pride and self-love:[2] "Husbands, love your wives, as Christ also loved the church, and delivered himself up for it:"[3] Thus this call to Christian patriarchy is essentially a call to love God and others unto the sacrificial death of self.[4]

The following pages maintain that today is the day for the advent of a new Christian patriarchy: a patriarchy deriving solely from Christ's own kingship. Because of the grave familial crisis of the time, such a patriarchy must necessarily be strong and pure. Indeed, in light of the critically debilitated state of Western manhood today such a patriarchy is necessarily miraculous. It is hoped that this book, in spite of its inadequacies and by God's grace, will clearly and compellingly issue the challenge and call to Christian patriarchy. For if Catholic men do not begin to answer this divine call of our age, there will be no essential rejuvenation of the family or restoration of the Church; that is, there will be no possibility for the advent of a new Christendom.

The doctrinal kernel of this manuscript (found in chapter two), along with the critical analysis of Pope John Paul

---

2. "The terms *pride* and *self-love* are used . . . somewhat interchangeably, for they are part and parcel of each other. Pride entails turning away from God to turn toward self—both apostasy and selfishness. This selfishness entails the seeking of one's own temporal pleasure, which is called cupidity. All vice springs from pride and self-love or *cupidity*." Dilsaver, G.C. (2008). *Imago Dei Psychotherapy*, p. 108.

3. Eph. 5:25.

4. This death to self essentially entails a dying to the *pseudo-self* that comprises "pride and self-love" and their ensuing personality defenses. *Ibid*, p. 105, 183.

II's writings (in appendix one), began to be developed while I was in the final stages of my graduate studies at the John Paul II Pontifical Institute for Studies on Marriage and Family. At the time, the faculty afforded me the singular opportunity to present a lecture on the patriarchal hierarchy of the family. In this lecture I asserted that the patriarchal hierarchy of the family was a constant and still-applicable teaching of the Church that is tantamount to an infallible teaching of the ordinary Magisterium. This assertion was not then, nor has it been since, doctrinally refuted.

CHAPTER 1

The Call to Christian Patriarchy

DARK TIMES, arguably the darkest of times in the annals of Christianity, have descended on both Faith and family at the eclipsed dawn of the twenty-first century. A full blown spiritual plague now rampages through the West and beyond. Pernicious and highly infectious, this plague is promulgated by governmental policies and commercial interests, and its pathogens ride the ubiquitous airwaves of the mass media and incubate in the passive minds of modern men.

This plague symptomatically erupts in materialism, hedonism, consumerism, and the myriad of personal sins. It is more lethal than any of Christianity's ancient heathen antagonists, for this new plague was cultivated over the centuries in the very matrix of Christianity, thereby mutating into a virulent strain that both mimics and resists the Gospel. Indeed, its proliferation is fueled by compromising and debilitating the body of Christ.

It is the plague of an anti-Catholic secularism and liberalism, and as it spreads the Faith recedes. In its wake the Church has experienced an unprecedented watering-down of the Faith to the point of heresy, a secular attrition where Catholics simply cease to practice their religion,[1] and a hemorrhaging loss of

---

1. Thirty-two percent of adult Americans who were raised Catholic have left the Church, and 10.1 percent of all American adults are ex-Catholics. Mainline Protestantism has fared even worse, going from sixty-six percent of the U.S. population fifty years ago to just eighteen percent. (*Faith in flux: Changes in religious affiliation in the U.S.* The Pew Forum on Religion & Public Life, April 2009.) However, Catholic affiliation was established in this survey by a person's

1

the faithful, in both domestic and mission fields, to aggressive secular Christian and pseudo-Christian sects.[2] Nor has history ever witnessed the breadth and depth of familial decimation occurring today: where marriage, even on the natural level, is distorted almost beyond recognition, and where the family is eviscerated of its ancient authority and stripped of its sacrosanct status.

If there is to be a wholesome future for the West, if Christianity is once again to make inroads into a heathen world, then the Christian family must be miraculously restored. For it is the family that will produce the saints of tomorrow: be they bishops, priests, religious, fathers or mothers. And it is the Christian family that is on the front lines of today's conflict between good and evil: it bears the brunt of that battle as the very last defense against the total domination of the secular and the profane.

Statistics chart the rapid and terminal decomposition of the

---

willingness to being identified as "Catholic" regardless of their specific beliefs and regardless of regular Mass attendance. Only a minority of these self-described "Catholics" are regular church-goers and only a quarter make the minimum "Easter duty" of annual Confession (Center for Applied Research in the Apostolate at Georgetown University, 2008). Even fewer still of these so claimed "Catholics" assent to all of the Church's moral teachings. Thus these statistics greatly overestimate the size of the authentic Catholic population, and greatly underestimate the severity of the great apostasy that has occurred in the Church over the last half-century.

2. Most forms of Protestantism are inherently secular, at least at the ideological level, due to their compartmentalization of faith from works, of church from state, of grace from an incarnational manifestation of sanctity. Although many evangelical sects today rail against the inroads of secularism it is the Protestant Reformation itself that laid the groundwork for it. Pseudo-Christian religions are those that claim the title of Christian yet reject the dogmatic definitions of Christology enunciated by the early Councils of the Catholic Church (Protestants themselves are forced to ascribe to these definitions in order to draw a line between themselves and the Pseudo-Christian cults). The Church of Latter-Day Saints and the Jehovah Witnesses are the largest of these Pseudo-Christian cults.

family in the United States. From 1970 to 1989 the divorce rate rose more than forty percent, since 1940 by 250 percent. In 1960 only five percent of all births were out of wedlock; by 1985 out-of-wedlock births had climbed to twenty-two percent (a number deflated by the 1.5 million babies murdered in the womb that year by legal abortion). In 1960 more than eighty percent of married women with children under six devoted themselves exclusively to domestic duties; by 1980 these home-makers were in the minority. In 1977, nearly eighty percent of America's children lived with both parents. Now, only two-thirds of them do. Of all families with children, nearly twenty-nine percent are now one-parent families, up from seventeen percent in 1977. Finally, from 1970 to 2004 the annual num-ber of marriages per 1,000 adult women in the United States plunged by nearly fifty percent.[3]

Of the many malignancies generated by the plague of anti-Christian and anti-God forces, what specific one metastasized within this most basic living unit of society? And what antidotal Christian principle will most directly attack this malignancy while providing the specific tonic to rejuvenate the wasted fam-ily? Though many factors have facilitated the destruction of the family, the final and proximate cause is to be found in the jettisoning of its essential structural order; that is, the rejection of the patriarchal hierarchy of the family, in the name of eman-cipation and egalitarianism. Therefore the restoration of the family, indeed the restoration of ecclesiastical leadership and Christendom itself, is only possible with the advent of a new Christian patriarchal order: the fatherly rule of family, com-munity, and Church.

3. U.S. Bureau of the Census, *Historical Statistics of the United States, Colonial Times to 1970* (Washington D.C.: U.S. Government Printing Office, 1975), 1:20, 64; U.S. Bureau of the Census, *Statistical Abstract of the United States: 1988*, 108th ed. (Washington D.C.: U.S. Government Printing Office, 1987), 59, 62, 83, 373, 374.

That Christian patriarchy is the specific antidote to the rampaging evils of the day is manifest in that there is no other Christian principle that so contradicts, so witnesses to, and hence so enrages, today's secular sensibilities. It is Christian patriarchy with its transcending authority that directly denies the secular state's assertion that *it* is the all-powerful, singular authority. It is Christian patriarchy with its requirements of personal sacrifice and lifelong commitment to others that so contradicts the West's self-centered individualism. It is Christian patriarchy with its emphasis on familial and religious duty that countermands today's constant agitation for assertion of personal rights. It is Christian patriarchy with its constant and unchanged ideals of two thousand years that rebuts today's invented standards of political correctness. And it is this principle that strikes at the very heart of the Western blight of emasculation and the corresponding pestilence of feminism: ills that eat away at the familial and traditional foundations of society and have as their most malicious fruit the atrocity of legal abortion.

Moreover, it is the principle of Christian patriarchy that today best speaks to the Church herself; for it is a principle that not only applies to husbands and familial fathers, but to all Christian men, and most certainly to priests and bishops. For it is Christian patriarchal fatherhood, with its requirements of magnanimous leadership and sacrificial service, that perfects manhood. The call to Christian patriarchy is simultaneously a call to Catholic womanhood, beckoning the daughters of the Church back to the ideal of the cloister, home, or convent and to the hidden life of maternal and spousal sanctification.

The re-establishing of a Christian patriarchy, no matter how quiet and domestic the implementation, will require heroic virtue. For this establishment will entail not only a confrontation with contemporary secular society, but a confrontation with the very fury of Hell, which is already fully engaged in a demonic blitzkrieg against fatherhood, motherhood, the unborn, and the traditional family. Although it is certain that no matter the ferocity of the enemy the gates of Hell shall not prevail against this Holy Church, in order to meet today's unprecedented challenge the Christian patriarchal order of the family established *must itself be unprecedented.* Indeed, the Christian patriarchy must be a new order purified of all selfish motives or worldly modes of brute dominance and based for the first time *solely* on Christ and His divine commission.

If such an order is established a new Christendom, be it small or great, will follow. Such a Christendom will be steadfast and transcendent, unswayed by the political currents and power curves of the world, because it will be rooted in the sacramental unit of the family and in the sanctified souls of the faithful.

Yet never before has there been a generation of men so unsuited to the establishing of an authentic Christian patriarchy. The Western male in particular, the erstwhile head of Christian culture, is found to have pawned his patriarchy for pleasure. He is thoroughly inculcated in the values of extended adolescence, and even where he rejects certain extremes of "playboyism," he has nonetheless, as a whole, acquiesced to the assaults of an hedonistic, immodest, and pornographic society; to the dominating search for pleasure and entertainment; to the beckon of a consumeristic society and the sophisticated toys it proffers; to contracepting his seed; and to the shirking of his duty to lead, protect, and provide for the family.

Yes, Christian men, and in particular the Western male who once was the standard-bearer of Christendom, has become satiated and complacent. He has allowed the state to intrude into the once-sacrosanct domain of the family, to the extent that the marriage bond itself has become less binding than even casual oral business contracts, severable by mere request. He has stood by while his wife serves the corporation and state, relegating home and family to a secondary concern. He has caused himself to be, in effect, castrated by vasectomy. He has permitted his offspring to be murdered in the womb. As each generation of men succeeds the previous one, the vestigial image of Christian manhood becomes less and less discernible The result is that both the Church and the Christian family have been emasculated. For the most part, even remnant orthodox Catholic families are matriarchies; as such the Church, emasculated at the familial and parish level, is quite unable to give appropriate and effective battle to the demonic forces aligned against her.

The Divine Response to the Times

Whether it is a case of his abdication or his usurpation, the Western Christian male has been soundly deposed in his role as father, leader, protector, and patriarch in a society that is maliciously and increasingly anti-Christian and anti-family. How then is a new and deeper understanding of fatherhood and patriarchy to be brought about in a day when Christian manhood is at its lowest ebb? How is this new order to be implemented when society is so set against it and where there is a dearth of role models and mentors—father figures who live out the call to manhood in its fullness—able to issue the call to the next generation?

The new and deeper understanding will be drawn from the unchangeable deposit of the Christian Faith, and the moral power to embrace and implement the ideals and duties of fatherhood will be imbued by supernatural grace.

Indeed, it is by *very reason* of the present unprecedented destruction of the family and the debilitation of manhood that this is the age of the Christian family and the Christian patriarch. For the Almighty in His economy of grace confounds evil by turning its greatest apparent triumphs into its greatest defeats: from Adam's tragic Fall, which the *Exultet* calls "happy,"[4] to that dark Friday when God Himself was crucified, which is called "good." It is this economy of grace that topples the mighty and proud by raising up the lowly and weak, thus making it perfectly clear that the power of God, not men, is at work. "Where sin abounded, grace did more abound."[5] Yes, it is precisely because there has never been a time so desperately in need of men able to answer the call to Christian patriarchy, nor a time when there has ever been such an unsuitable selection of these men, that Christians may justifiable expect an unparalleled outpouring of God's miraculous grace and favor on Christian manhood, and on the family he is called to lead.

Mirroring God's economy of grace is the Church's response to the crises of the times. Throughout the history of the Church, specific dogmas and morals have been defined, defended, and emphasized when the corollary heresy or immorality reached proportions that required it. Today, when there is confusion about even the most elementary and essential characteristics of sexual identity, the Church is called to define truths about family, fatherhood, and motherhood—truths that never needed defining or defending before.

Historic Western Patriarchy

Historically, in the Christian West patriarchy needed little definition or defense: it was integrated into the already existing patriarchal structure of the Greco-Roman world. Bolstered by the social, political, and economic order, the patriarchy of an emerging Christendom was never socially or philosophically

---

4. "O happy fault . . . which gained for us so great a Redeemer."
5. Rom. 5:20

challenged and hence was never forced to define itself on a purely
Christian basis. As a result, the patriarchy of the Christianized
West remained to some degree anchored to enduring pagan
patriarchal stays, and tainted by pagan values. In that patriarchy
was the pervasive political and social order of the West, and
since the understanding and practice of patriarchy continued to
be in many ways based on a pagan model, the *political* and *social*
order of the West remained to some extent based on principles
that were other than those of the gospel.

In accord with its incarnating nature, from the remnants of
a decaying civilization and a mixture of diverse and barbaric
peoples, Catholicism created the matchless culture that was
Europe. Most amazingly, it did so under the unifying tutelage
of the papacy, whose initial and final only real instruments
of influence and government were of a spiritual and moral
nature. Nonetheless—and without diminishing the unparalleled, indeed miraculous achievements of Christendom—one
may still question whether or not Europe was as Catholic as
it could have been. Most specifically one may question the
Catholic quality and integrity of its political and social order
(as distinct from its spiritual order and cultural manifestations)
which ended up being soundly vanquished from the world
scene (made all the more mournful due to the present political
resurgence of Islam). One may wonder how the Crusades could
ultimately and shamefully fail. Or how it was that at medieval
Christendom's apex, Catholic countries still fought Catholic
countries. Or how it was that during the Reformation, Catholic
kings aligned themselves with Protestant princes against other
Catholic kings. Or how these so-called Catholic kingdoms
failed to ever truly unite in Christ? Even during the late Middle
Ages, when a brief semblance of internal secular peace was
achieved and its princes united in a common crusade with King
St. Louis IX—the personification of Christian chivalry—the

hierarchy of the Church was rife with the political intrigues and infighting of her own princes: there were popes and antipopes, and more than once the Chair of Peter was left scandalously vacant for years at a time, due to an inability of politically motivated cardinals to agree on a successor.

These societal and ecclesiastical failings occurred because Christendom was still based too much on a worldly power structure; because its power structure adopted as its leadership prototype a sanitized version of pagan patriarchy rather than a purely Christian one. The fact that a pagan patriarchal structure was very much present in Christendom is witnessed to most glaringly and to the point by the double standard of sexual mores[6] that remained embedded in all of the ancient

---

6. It must be noted that while a "double standard" of sexual license is totally unacceptable in Christian morality, it still remains better than the present standard where both genders are given equal sexual license. In fact the double standard has some basis in natural law. St. Thomas Aquinas wrote that a man having "a plurality of wives neither wholly destroys nor in anyway hinders the first end of marriage [i.e. according to natural law "the begetting and rearing of offspring"], since one man is sufficient to get children of several wives, and to rear the children born of them . . . Whereas, for one wife to have several husbands is contrary to the first principles of natural law, since thereby the good of the offspring which is the principle end of marriage is, in one respect, entirely destroyed, and in another respect hindered. Now the begetting of offspring, though not wholly voided,* is nevertheless considerably hindered . . . But the rearing of offspring is altogether done away, because as a result of one woman having several husbands there follows uncertainty of the offspring in relation to its father, whose care is necessary for its education. Wherefore the marriage of one wife with several husbands has not been sanctioned by any law or custom, whereas the converse has been." (Suppl. Q. 65, Art. 1). Though a double standard does not contravene the primary end of marriage, nonetheless, it hinders other natural goods of marriage (of these St. Thomas mentions "fidelity") and, of course, is essentially antithetical to Christian marriage and patriarchy (see Chapter VII). Also note well that St. Thomas is commenting on polygamous marriage among non-Christian people. In regards to any form of concubinage (the polygamous arrangement that was and is prevalent, even socially acceptable, in Christian cradle civilizations) he states that it is always against natural law since it does not sufficiently

cradle cultures of Christianity. In the age of chivalry, the age most identified with Catholic manhood, the aristocracy (lords and knights, indeed clergy and bishops) were allowed great sexual license. Even "divorce-annulment" (the granting of an annulment on invalid grounds) was available to the aristocracy depending on their positions of power: church authorities, in practice, acquiescing to their worldly influence. Finally, it was specifically this failure of Christian manhood to live out the principle of marital exclusivity that fueled the great breakup of Christianity itself: as Henry VIII rebelled at an uncharacteristically staunch enforcement of the Christian marital law[7] and the

---

provide for the proper rearing of offspring. (Suppl. Q. 65 Art. 3). Still as grace builds upon nature (or the supernatural law upon the natural law), Christian propriety does call for a double standard of comportment in which a woman is expected to behave with a degree of modesty and reserve which if practiced by a man would be considered effeminate. Still, a man is held to a standard that, while not effeminate, is Christian and edifying.

* St. Thomas was of the Aristotelian belief that a woman already pregnant could become impregnated a second time (in fact, second, simultaneous pregnancies can occur, though they are extremely rare). Hence, his argument in light of today's knowledge of feminine fertility would "wholly void" the first respect of "begetting offspring"; for not only is a woman as a rule unable to become impregnated during pregnancy, but it is only an approximate 3-5 days (24 hrs of which she is actually fertile) out of her monthly cycle that intercourse can possibly result in conception. Hence, in accord with the most primary end of begetting children, polyandry is biologically squanderous. From a purely biological aim of procreating, polygamy is most efficient; since a man is fertile even during a woman's monthly infertile periods, pregnancy, and menopausal stage.

7. Though Pope Clement VII may be said to have been influenced greatly by political pressure (his desire to avoid offending Spain, since Catherine was the daughter of Ferdinand and Isabella) in his refusal of Henry VIII's request for annulment, this earth-shaking ruling was nonetheless providential, a grand example of the Holy Spirit's directing of the Church regardless of the less than pristine motives of men. For the granting of an annulment would have been a blatant about face after Rome had specifically ruled that Henry could marry Catherine on the grounds that her marriage to Henry's brother had never been consummated. Though England was tragically lost, the Church's marital decrees and practices began to conform consistently with her doctrine on marriage. Had the

hapless monk Luther found himself unable to live a chaste life. The question must be asked by those still unconvinced: would a truly integral Christendom that was fully and firmly established as the power structure of the West suffer such inglorious defeat and then simply wither away? The fact that the marital principles of Christian patriarchy were never integrally embraced by the aristocracy gives credence to the assertion that the principles of hierarchical order, likewise, did not integrally permeate the power structure of the West. Thus one may venture to say that the erstwhile Christendom of the West (that is, its political and social power structure), though tempered and influenced by the Christian ethos, remained too pagan at heart. Even if one asserts (and quite defensibly) that Christendom at its zenith was the very zenith of all history, it was nonetheless still insufficient to stem the disintegration of the West into its present anti-Christian character.

The insufficiency of Christendom has nothing to do with any lack in the truths and ideals of Catholicism, but rather with men and their failure to apply them. This failure is specifically a failure of Christian patriarchy. Recognizing that princes and prelates, husbands and fathers, too often pursued their own self-gratification and personal gain instead of personal sanctity and the good of the Church and their charges is only to be cognizant of the fallen nature of man. But for men imbued with the

---

Pope acquiesced to Henry, who continued his serial polygamy way beyond any semblance of even pagan propriety, the Church's teaching authority in regards to holy Matrimony would have been badly compromised, and Henry's continual suings for annulment would have eventually been denied if only to avoid a farce.

The granting of annulments, which in theory does not contradict the doctrine of indissolubility, is nonetheless very susceptible to laxity and abuses, being dependent on the testimony of the petitioner and the juridical judgment of canons. Though England was lost, the Church's integrity and teaching credibility on the indissolubility of marriage was saved, and she stands alone today as the sole defender of the unseverable bonds of marriage.

militant spirit of Catholicism, such a recognition of their ances-
tors' deficiencies is also a challenge to engage in a corporate
pursuit of a new Christendom, and a double reminder of their
own much greater deficiencies as they strive to surpass their
own personal past in the pursuit of sanctity. Audacious though
it may sound (but audacious in Christ), today's generation of
Catholic men must begin to envision a new Christendom that is
not only judged and spurred on by the accomplishments of the
old, but seeks to surpass them. This new Christendom will be
based essentially on a Christ-centered patriarchy, the personal
pursuit of sanctity, and the advancement of Faith and family.

A New Christian Patriarchy

Today's Western culture lacks societal structures to uphold
patriarchal authority; indeed, its structures and values are radically opposed to any such authority. The natural, pagan patriarchy of the West has crumbled, based as it was too much upon
a temporal foundation. But with the final disintegration of the
West's ancient patriarchal structure comes the opportunity to
build a new patriarchy that is based solely on Christ, deriving its
authority solely from His commission, and finding its strength
in the adherence to the Gospel and specifically to the vows of
Holy Matrimony. Such a patriarchy must be imbued with the
witnessing militancy of the Church, and, like the Church herself—which has lost its temporal power and now finds herself
reduced to her essential and indefectible nature as a spiritual
power—the seminal new Christian patriarchy finds itself without societal, cultural, or even, in many ways, natural structures
to facilitate its establishment.

Secular society's hostility toward patriarchy goes hand in
hand with its devaluation of motherhood—traditionally considered the essence of feminine character—and its degradation

of the family. But the intelligentsia of the twentieth century have focused their primary attack on the father figure. Freud said that culture began with "patricide." Mitscherlich asserted that contemporary civilization has progressed into "a fatherless society." And politically we have been told that "emancipation" from patriarchal structures is, according to Marx, a "restoration of humanity and of human relations."

The resultant ideology of the intelligentsia, in which the term "patriarchy" is strictly a pejorative and where fatherhood is dead, inevitable finds its way to the mass media and other organs of popular culture. Hence, for example, it is the father who on television is most often targeted for parody or made to play the role of the buffoon. Especially targeted is the father in the form of the Western male (usually stereotyped as the male of European descent), whose forebears were the very fathers of Christian civilization. Very rarely, unless he is to be satirized or villainized in the role, is the Western male given a position of authority, wisdom, or strength. The strategy is clear: cut off the head and the body will wither. By once and for all deposing the traditional Western leader, the Christian father, traditional Western Christian culture will likewise wither away—once and for all.

The Catholic clergy, representing both theistic and ecclesiastical authority, has also earned the hatred of a world opposed to fatherhood. It was the clergy, by exploits of unparalleled heroism, that spread the seeds of the Faith far and wide and brought Christian civilization to fruition. However, the ranks of the clergy have also entailed Judas priests and bishops who have betrayed Christ and His holy Church with the effeminization[8] of some men in the priesthood, contributing greatly to the

---

8. The very lowest estimate is that 81% of the cases were of a homosexual nature. John Jay College of Criminal Justice (2004). *The Nature and Scope of the Problem of Sexual Abuse of Minors by Catholic Priests and Deacons in the United States.* New York.

scandal that currently surrounds the Church. Today there is an urgent need for prophetic and courageous priests and bishops of pristine fatherly character to witness to the true nature of their office; and, again, it is the family that holds the key to their advent, for the home is the first seminary, and the familial father is the primary role model for the future Reverend Father.

The world's hatred of the priesthood and Magisterium is obvious and to be expected, but sadly, even within the Church some hold the firm conviction that this God-ordain magisterial order is oppressive and dysfunctional and must be cleansed of its patriarchal aspects, if not done away with altogether.

The Age of the Family

If a new Christian patriarchy is to arise, it must do so from the ranks of the laity. It is in keeping with the divine economy of grace, which answers evil with timely charisms and their ensuing apostolic movements, that today's age is truly the "age of the laity." Not as misconstrued by those egalitarians who seek to empower the laity to supplant the ordained authority, but rather in the sense that it is the age of the *family*: the institution in which the lay state is sanctified and perfected. As the traditional Christian family faces its apparent demise, as motherhood is relegated to a secondary status and Christian manhood is at best a parody, as confusion reigns even in regards to sexual identity, Christ demarcates this time as the hour of the family: of motherhood and the home, and of the Christian patriarch. Today the faithful can expect the advent of a new Christian familial order that re-affirms, further defines, and enhances the ancient truths. And it is the laity that must do so, for the *ecclesia domestica* is their sphere of authority and competency.

The patriarchs of old led the chosen people through the vicissitudes of salvation history. St. Joseph led the Holy Family through the dark and murderous nights of their desert escape. The Magisterium has led the Church to withstand heresies and schisms and the ceaseless siege of the world. And now, as the forces of darkness rage against the once-sacrosanct and indomitable institution of the family, chosen men are again called to rise up and wield with manly fortitude and love the singular staff of patriarchy: a staff that is at one and the same time *Scepter, Crosier,* and *Cross.* Such is the commission of Christ in these times of dark crisis to those that would lead the Church and the family in His stead until He comes again in glory.

Chapter 2

The Family is a Patriarchal Hierarchy

Especially in today's pervasive atmosphere of hyper-egalitarianism, the acceptance of the hierarchical structure of the Church's magisterial priesthood is a *sine qua non* for Catholics. Any credible claimant to Catholic orthodoxy must accept the Church's teaching and ruling authority, no matter how ranging and otherwise incongruous other issues may be.

But there is another God-ordained hierarchical structure that is part and parcel of the orthodox corpus. Like its ecclesiastical counterpart, it is patriarchal; but unlike ecclesiastical patriarchy, considered the lowest common denominator of orthodoxy, this patriarchy is the most divisive of orthodox concepts. For there is nothing that so contradicts the contemporary ethos of hyper-egalitarianism as the patriarchal hierarchy of the family: the teaching that prescribes a man's spiritual and juridical headship over his wife and children.

Patriarchy in the Preternatural State

Contrary to the wishes of some contemporary theologians, Christ came not to eradicate the patriarchal order, but to elevate it, just as He elevated and restored marriage as a whole to its original preternatural understanding. Indeed, the preternatural familial state as recorded in Genesis is unintelligible without the understanding of its patriarchal principle. Adam is placed among creation as "the image of God," thus becoming His very representative. "Just as powerful earthly kings, to indicate their claim to dominion, erect an image of themselves in the provinces of their empire where they do not personally appear, so man is placed upon earth in God's image as God's sovereign emblem."[1]

Adam's commission to name the animals is also significant. "The superiority of man over the beasts is shown by his naming them [Gen. 2:19-20]. In the ancient world to give a name was a sign of authority."[2] Adam authority over Eve was also indicated by his twice naming her, both before and after the Fall. "And Adam said: This now is bone of my bones, and flesh of my flesh; she shall be called woman, because she was taken out of man."[3] "And Adam called the name of his wife Eve: because she was the mother of all the living."[4] And it was Adam alone who, as patriarchal representative, was called to by God after the couple had eaten of the tree. "And the Lord God called Adam, and said to him: Where art thou?"[5] Indeed, Adam's negligence in protecting and guiding Eve, resulting in her encounter with the serpent, and his subsequent following of her lead, are the primal sins of omission and commission against patriarchy and its order.

Most importantly, for gleaning the patriarchal significance of the creation account, is the Church's doctrinal understanding of it. Indeed, the Church's pivotal dogma of original sin is predicated on Adam's patriarchal status before the Fall. It is from Adam alone that original sin was incurred. "As through *one man*," St. Paul says, "Wherefore as by *one man*," St. Paul says, "sin entered into this world, and by sin death...[and] as by

---

1. Gerhard von Rad, *Genesis*, 3rd rev. ed. (London: SCM Press, 1972), p.60.
2. John L. McKenzie, S.J., *Dictionary of the Bible*, (Milwaukee, The Bruce Publishing Company, 1965), p.12.
3. Gen. 2:23 .
4. Gen. 3:20.
5. Gen. 3:9.

the *offence of one*, unto all men to condemnation; so also by the justice of one, unto all men to justification of life." (emphasis mine)[6] St. Augustine stated that "the deliberate sin of the first man is the cause of original sin."[7] The Church without exception premises all its doctrinal statements concerning original sin on its cause being the personal sin of Adam, not because it was the first human sin (that sin was committed by Eve) but because it was committed by the person who was the origin of the human race.[8] If only Eve had sinned, then only she would have experienced the consequences of that sin. But when

---

6. Rom. 5:12, 18.

7. De Nuptiis et Concupiscentiâ, II, xxvi, 43. "Deliberate sin" is necessarily personal, that is, committed by an individual.

8. In the Church's teaching of the doctrine of original sin against heretical propositions, she takes as a given that original sin derives solely from Adam as the head of the human race. The Council of Orange (529), confirmed by Boniface II, declared that "If anyone asserts that Adam's sin was injurious only to Adam and not to his descendants, or if he declares that it was only the death of the body which is punishment for sin, and not the sin, the death of the soul, that passed from *one* man to all the human race, he attributes an injustice to God and contradicts the words of the Apostle, 'Through *one* man sin entered into the world, and through sin death, and thus death has passed into all men because all have sinned'" (*DB* 175). The Council of Trent declared, "If anyone says that *this sin of Adam, which is one by origin* and is communicated to all by propagation and not by imitation (*propagatione, non imitatione*), and is in all and proper to each, (if anyone says) that it can be taken away through the powers of human nature or by some other remedy than through the merit of the one mediator, our Lord Jesus Christ, . . . or denies that this merit of Jesus Christ is applied through the sacrament of baptism both to adults as well as to infants . . . let him be anathema" (Fifth Session, Canon Three). The late Fr. John A. Hardon, S.J., sums up, "Adam is alone identified as the author of original sin, though Scripture clearly shows Eve as his accomplice and, in fact, the one who tempted her husband. Yet because the [Church] documents confine themselves to Adam we also limit our statement of responsibility to the first man" (*God the Author of Nature and the Supernatural*, Part II: Creation as a Divine Fact, Section Two: Supernatural Anthropology; THESIS VII, Adam was an Individual Man, From Whom the Whole Human Race Derives Its Origin). Retrieved from http://www.therealpresence.org/archives/God/God_012.htm

Adam sinned—as patriarch, head, and representative of the human race—the consequences affected all his descendants, the entire human race.

In seeming answer to all those Christian socialists who would advance their Utopian fantasies by portraying humanity before the Fall as classless and totally egalitarian, St. Thomas Aquinas wrote (in answer to the question, "Whether in the state of innocence man would have been master over man?"), "The condition of man in the state of innocence was not more exulted than the condition of the angels. But among the angels some rule over others; and so one order is called *Dominations*. Therefore, it was not beneath the dignity of the state of innocence that one man should be subject to another."[9]

The principle of patriarchy would also permeate the entirety of Hebrew culture and spirituality. From the absolute social and spiritual rule of the ancient patriarchs, to Abraham's covenant made in the name of his posterity, to the institution of the Israelite priesthood, to the specifically male duty of study and prayer, to the ministerial role of the father in the religious services of the home, the principle of patriarchy has characterized the full span of Hebrew salvation history and spirituality. So too, the "merits of the fathers" is an ancient concept, predating and much repeated in rabbinical literature, that stresses the continual blessings of the patriarchs. An example of this is Moses, who himself is acting as an intercessor, evoking the past merits of the fathers in behalf of the Israelites when they fell to worshiping the golden calf: "let thy anger cease, and be appeased upon the wickedness of thy people. Remember Abraham, Isaac, and Israel, thy servants"[10] St. Paul, who as a youth studied under one of the great teachers of the law, Rabban Gamaliel, also employs this concept when he speaks

9. St. Thomas Aquinas, *Summa Theologica*, Pt. I, Q. 96, Art. 4.
10. Ex. 32:12-13.

of the Jews as still loved by God, loved "for the sake of the Fathers."[11]

Patriarchy in Ancient Paganism

Just as the truth of the matter is quite the opposite of the contention that Christ's restoration and elevation of marriage did away with patriarchy, so too is it a diametrical falsehood that the nascent Church was merely aping the culture of her times when she advanced the teaching of patriarchy and the submission of women. Indeed, as the Church expanded into gentile society she found herself in a morally decaying milieu much like that of the twentieth-century West, where an *atmosphere of paganism, a tendency toward egalitarianism, and an ascendancy of feminism* pervaded. Pope Pius XII summarized the domestic disintegration of the pagan milieu into which Christianity was born as follows:

> In the [ancient] Roman world, notwithstanding the respect and dignity surrounding the mother of the family, she was withal according to ancient law, juridically subject to her husband or *paterfamilias*, who had supreme power in the home. But with the passing of the centuries, the laws of the ancients concerning the family fell into disuse; their iron discipline disappeared, and women became practically independent of the authority of the husband. Doubtless there remained shining examples of excellent wives and mothers, imitators of the matrons of old . . . but opposed to such irreproachable personalities there arose in vivid contrast the ever growing number of women, especially of high society, who fled disdainfully from the duties of motherhood to give themselves rather to occupations and to play a part till then reserved to men alone. At the same time, as divorce multiplied, the

---

11. Rom. 11:28.

family began to disintegrate, and womanly affections and behavior deviated from the straight path of virtue to such an extent that it drew from Seneca the bitter lament: "Does there now remain any woman at all who is ashamed to break her marriage . . . when they divorce to remarry, and marry only to divorce?"[12]

Pius XII goes on to conclude: "To reestablish in the family that hierarchy indispensable for unity and happiness, and at the same time to restore the original and true grandeur of conjugal love, was one of the greatest undertakings of Christendom."[13] Hence, St. Paul was not merely reiterating cultural principles of his time, he was in fact witnessing *against* the currents of his time when he set out to reestablish and elevate the patriarchal hierarchy of the family.

Patriarchy in the Catholic Tradition

Pope Pius XII states in the same allocution that

the Christian concept of matrimony which St. Paul taught to his disciples of Ephesus, just as he did to those of Corinth, could not be clearer or more forthright: "Let women be subject to their husbands, as to the Lord: Because the husband is the head of the wife, as Christ is the head of the church … as the church is subject to Christ, so also let the wives be to their husbands in all things. Husbands, love your wives, as Christ also loved the church, and delivered himself up for it … let every one of you in particular love his wife as himself: and let the wife fear her husband."[14] What is this doctrine and teaching of Paul if not the teaching and doctrine

---

12. Pius XII, "*Allocution to Newly-Weds*," September 10, 1941, para. 74.
13. *Ibid.,* para. 78.
14. 14. Eph. 5:22, 25, 33..

of Christ? The divine Redeemer came thus to restore what paganism had overthrown.[15]

Elsewhere in Scripture, the preeminent epistles of St. Peter and St. Paul are quite clear on the teaching of hierarchy of the family, as indicated from excerpts of their pastoral letters. The Prince of the Apostles gives Christian women an example of their proper relationship with their husbands: "For after this manner heretofore the holy women also, who trusted in God, adorned themselves, being in subjection to their own husbands: As Sara obeyed Abraham, calling him lord"[16]

Elsewhere the Apostle admonishes women "To be discreet, chaste, sober, having a care of the house, gentle, obedient to their husbands, that the word of God be not blasphemed."[17] and reminds his flock that just as "the head of every man is Christ; and the head of the woman is the man."[18]

As Pius XII noted, the Christianization of the Greco-Roman world infused that society's ancient patriarchal structure with new vigor. Since the writings of the Church Fathers were, like the decrees and definitions of the Church, prompted primarily by controversy they do not include detailed doctrinal defenses of patriarchal hierarchy of the family; this principle was a given, both of natural law and Divine Revelation. Their writings do, however, speak of the Christian spirit of this hierarchy, wherein a wife is subjected to her husband through the bonds of love rather than coercion. St. Chrysostom, commenting "that each one of you must love his wife as he loves himself; and let every wife fear her husband," and specifically on whether or not fear excludes love, remarks:

---

15. *Ibid.*
16. 1 Pet. 3:5-6.
17. Titus 2:5.
18. 1 Cor. 11:3

The wife is a secondary authority; let not her then demand equality, for she is under the head; nor let him despise her for being in subjection, for she is the body; and if the head despises the body it will itself also perish . . . For she that fears and reverences, loves also; and she that loves, fears, and reverences him as being the head, and loves him as being a member, since the head itself is the member of the body at large. Hence he [Christ] places the one in subjection the other in authority, that there may be peace; for where there is equal authority there can never be peace; neither where a house is a democracy, nor where all are rulers; but the ruling authority must of necessity be one.[19]

St. Ambrose, often quoted out of context as advocating against patriarchy, does admonish women to bear with their husbands, for "it is right that he whom the woman enticed to do wrong should assume the office of guide, lest he fall once more because of feminine instability," and goes on to admonish husbands to treat their spouses not as slaves but as wives: "Get rid of your obstinacy when your gentle consort offers you her love. You are not her master, but a husband. You have not acquired perchance a handmaid, but a wife. God designed you to be a guide to the weaker sex, not a dictator."[20] Yet elsewhere, in elaborating on the Fall, St. Ambrose writes: "She was first to be deceived and was responsible for deceiving the man. Wherefore the Apostle Paul has related that holy women have in olden times been subject to the stronger vessel and recommends them to obey their husbands as their *masters.*"[21]

Some progressive theologians have sought to use St. Ambrose's words, "You are not a master, but a husband" as

---

19. St. John Chrysostom, *Homilies on Ephesians*, Homily XX, ver. 26.
20. Saint Ambrose, *Six Days of Creation: Five*, Chapter VII, sec. 18-19.
21. Saint Ambrose, *Paradise*, Chapter IV, sec. 24.

evidence of a Church Father who did not support patriarchal hierarchy, but it is clear that in context St. Ambrose clearly accepts St. Paul exhortation that wives "obey their husbands as their masters." Indeed, elsewhere St. Ambrose is quite explicit in his view of a certain male superiority: "Although created outside of Paradise, that is in an inferior place, man is found to be superior, whereas woman, created in a better place, that is to say, in Paradise, is found to be inferior."[22] Although this passage is apt to be misconstrued as denying the intrinsic equal worth and dignity of women, it nonetheless definitely puts an end to the false notion that St. Ambrose opposed patriarchal hierarchy.

St. Augustine refers to the duties and nature of the hierarchical order in *The City of God*: "Domestic peace is the well-ordered concord between those of the family who rule and those who obey . . . Order is the distribution which allots things equal and unequal, each to its own place." St. Augustine goes on to elaborate on the domestic order:

> And this is the order of this concord, that a man, in the first place, injure no one, and, in the second, do good to everyone he can reach. Primarily, therefore, his own household are his care, for the law of nature and of society gives him readier access to them and greater opportunity of serving them . . . This is the origin of domestic peace, or the well ordered concord of those in the family who rule and those who obey. For they who care for the rest rule—the husband the wife, the parents the children, the masters the servants; and they who are cared for obey—the women their husbands, the children their parents, the servants their masters.[23]

---

22. *Ibid.*
23. St. Augustine, *The City of God*, bk. 19, ch. 14.

In its summation of fifteen hundred years of Church teaching, the *Roman Catechism* restated the doctrine of the patriarchal hierarchy of the family in these strong and unequivocal words: "Again, and in this the conjugal union chiefly consists, let wives never forget that next to God they are to love their husbands, to esteem them above all others, yielding to them in all things not inconsistent to Christian piety, a willing and ready obedience."[24]

The Magisterium of the Church continued to affirm this teaching after the post-Reformation upheaval of Western civilization. Pope Leo XIII, who witnessed the final dismantling of the *ancien regime* and the beginnings of the feminist movement, staunchly stated: "The husband is chief of the family, and the head of the wife. The woman, because she is flesh of his flesh and bone of his bone, must be subject to her husband and obey him."[25] A half-century later Pope Pius XI, who witnessed a triumphant feminist movement gain widespread acceptance for its other banner issue of artificial contraception, citing the teachings of St. Paul, St. Augustine, and Pope Leo XIII, proclaimed: "Domestic society being confirmed, therefore, by this bond of love, there should flourish in it that 'order of love,' as St. Augustine calls it. This order includes both the primacy of the husband with regard to the wife and children, the ready subjection of the wife and her willing obedience, which the Apostle commends. . ."[26] And finally, during the earth-shaking and society-shattering days of World War II, Pope Pius XII exhorted a gathering of newlywed wives to adhere to the clear teaching of the Church on the hierarchy of the family:

> Every family is a society; every well-ordered society needs

---

24. *Ibid.,* The Sacrament of Matrimony; "On the Duties of a Christian Wife."
25. Leo XIII, *Arcanum*, Encyclical letter, 10 Feb. 1880.
26. Pope Pius XI, *Casti Connubii*, Encyclical Letter, 1930.

a head; every power of headship comes from God. And so, too, the family you have founded has a head, invested with authority by God: authority over her who has been given him as a companion to constitute the nucleus of this family, and over those who with the Lord's blessing will come to swell it and make it happy, like young shoots from the bole of the olive."[27]

The Principle of Christian Patriarchal Hierarchy

Intimately connected with the principle of patriarchal hierarchy of the family are both the sacramentality of marriage and the foundation of ecclesiology. The Catechism of Trent states:

> When Christ our Lord wished to give a sign of the intimate union that exists between Him and His Church and His immense love for us, He chose especially the sacred union of man and wife . . . That Matrimony is a Sacrament of the Church, following the authority of the Apostle, has always held to be certain and incontestable.

This dual doctrine first enunciated by the Apostle in Ephesians 5, provides the Church with the basis for the hierarchy of marriage:

> Being subject one to another, in the fear of Christ. Let women be subject to their husbands, as to the Lord: Because the husband is the head of the wife, as Christ is the head of the church. He is the saviour of his body. Therefore as the *church is subject to Christ*, so also let the wives be to their husbands in all things. Husbands, love your wives, as Christ also loved the church, and delivered himself up for it: That he might sanctify it, cleansing it by the laver of water in the

---

27. Pius XII, *op. cit.*, para. 82.

word of life: That he might present it to himself a glorious church, not having spot or wrinkle, or any; such thing; but that it should be holy, and without blemish. So also ought men to love their wives as their own bodies. He that loveth his wife, loveth himself. For no man ever hated his own flesh; but nourisheth and cherisheth it, as also Christ doth the church: Because we are members of his body, of his flesh, and of his bones. For this cause shall a man leave his father and mother, and shall cleave to his wife, and they shall be two in one flesh. This is a great sacrament; but I speak in Christ and in the church. Nevertheless let every one of you in particular love his wife as himself: and let the wife fear her husband. "[28]

The Catechism of Trent goes on to teach that the phrase *this mystery has many implications*,

undoubtedly refers to Matrimony, and must be taken to mean that the union of man and wife, which has God for its Author, is a Sacrament [which is the Latin translation of the Greek word *mysterion* or "mystery"], that is, a sacred sign of that most holy union that binds Christ our Lord to His Church. That this is the true and proper meaning of the Apostle's words is shown by the ancient holy Fathers who have interpreted them, and by the explanation furnished by the Council of Trent. It is indubitable, therefore, that the Apostle compares the husband to Christ, and the wife to the Church; that the husband is head of the wife as Christ is the head of the Church.

Pope Pius XII comments as follows on the inseparable Pauline dual doctrine of the matrimonial sacrament and the hierarchy of the family:

---

28. Eph. 5:21-33.

In raising to the dignity of a sacrament marriage between baptized persons, Christ conferred on husband and wife an incomparable dignity, and gave to their union a redemptive function. When he affirms that wives must be subject to their husbands like the Church to Christ, St. Paul establishes a very clear difference between husband and wife, but at the same time, he illustrates the power of what joins them one to the other, and which renders indissoluble the bond of union."[29]

Hence, the sacramentality of marriage and the principle of familial hierarchy are intrinsically connected with one another, forming, as it were, a dual doctrine. To attempt to excise the principle of familial hierarchy from the body of Church teaching would require a radical reevaluation of the sacramentality and nature of marriage itself, which was developed doctrinally in integral union with the principle of familial hierarchy.

The signature traits of Christian marriage, indissolubility and exclusivity, both take as their principle the Pauline prototype of Christ and the Church and the expression of it in the relationship of man and wife. Those of a feminist bent who would like to do away with the Ephesians 5 passage, in order to do away with wifely submission, should keep in mind that this is the selfsame passage that is the basis for indissoluble, monogamous marriage (which is surely the greatest historical advance of women, and, indeed, has raised them up as no theory of emancipation has ever done). If it were possible to delete the doctrine of patriarchal familial hierarchy from the corpus of Church teachings, then the matrimonial doctrine on exclusivity, indissolubility, and indeed the very sacramentality of marriage itself, would need to be reconstructed.

---

29. Pope Pius XII, Allocution to the World Union of Catholic Women's Organizations, September 29, 1957.

The Certitude of Church Teaching on Patriarchy

Thus the sacramental understanding of marriage requires that it keep its character as a typification of Christ and the Church. This in itself would seem to render the hierarchical order of marriage an immutable characteristic of an orthodox theology of marriage because hierarchy is integral to the prototypical relationship of Christ and the Church. In addition, the Church has stated with its greatest authority and certitude (*de fide* pronouncement) that original sin was transmitted to the entire human race through the actions of one man, Adam. Thus the Church bases this pivotal dogma of original sin—the very reason for the Church and Christ's redemptive sacrifice—on Adam's patriarchal headship over the entire human family; Adam is the first father. Hence this pivotal dogmatic statement is dependent on the crucial spiritual reality of patriarchy in the preternatural state. The teaching of patriarchal authority, then, can be classified at least as a teaching pertaining to the Faith, and as such to be held as "theologically certain" (*sententia ad fidem pertinens, theologice certa*). Since Christ came to restore the original ideal of marriage, this must include the restoration of familial patriarchy and hierarchy.[30]

So too, the Magisterium has continued to reiterate and define the doctrine of the patriarchal hierarchy of the family for nearly two thousand years. That this doctrine has been both universally promulgated and universally accepted is witnessed to by its constant derivation from the Church's exegesis of Holy Scripture; by its promulgation by the Church Fathers; by its clear and forceful inclusion in the Roman Catechism issued by

---

30. Where Adam as the universal father had an authority that extended to all his descendants, that is, the entire human race, each father would proportionally have an authority over his own descendants, that is, his own family; taking into account, of course the universal ramifications of Adam's primary patriarchy that singularly established man's inherited spiritual disposition.

the dogmatic Council of Trent, and from which all subsequent catechisms till the post-Vatican II era were derived; and by its repeated teaching in doctrinal encyclicals and utterances of the Popes.

It appears then that this teaching has enjoyed for the vast majority of the Church's existence the status of a universal moral teaching and been accepted as such by both the hierarchy and the faithful. As such, it would seem to follow that this teaching is infallible. This status of infallibility would derive from the ordinary Magisterium[31] of the Church, which Vatican II explained thus: "Although the individual bishops do not enjoy the prerogative of infallibility, they do, nevertheless, enunciate the doctrine of Christ infallible when, even dispersed around the world but preserving the bond of communion between themselves and with the successor of Peter, they concur on one judgment as having to be held definitively, while authentically teaching on faith and morals."[32] According to the 1917 Code of Canon Law, ordinary teaching infallibility incurs when *one* of the following is displayed:

[1] The Bishops exercise their infallible teaching power in an ordinary manner when they, in moral unity with the Pope, unanimously promulgate the same teachings on faith and morals. [2] The [First] Vatican Council expressly declared that also the truths of Revelation [i.e. Holy Scripture] proposed as such by the ordinary and general teaching office of the Church are to be firmly held with "divine and catholic faith." The incumbents of the ordinary and general teaching office of the Church are the members of the whole

31. In proposing a teaching of faith or morals as one to be held by all the faithful, the totality of the Bishops, in union with the Pope, exercise infallibility both in an *extraordinary manner*, when they are assembled in a general council, and in an *ordinary manner*, when scattered over the earth.

32. Documents of Vatican II, Lumen Gentium, 25.

episcopate scattered over the whole earth. [3] The agreement of the Bishops in doctrine may be determined from the catechisms issued by them . . . [4] A morally general agreement suffices, but in this the express or tacit assent of the Pope, as the supreme head of the episcopate, is essential.[33]

The doctrine of the patriarchal hierarchy of the family appears to fit *all four* means for designating a teaching infallible in an ordinary manner (the issuance of the promulgation of the Catechism of Trent, a universal dogmatic catechism that was also universally promulgated by the episcopate, would suffice for the third means).

The wording of Vatican's II statement taken by itself, and as formulated by post-conciliar theologians, produces a slightly different emphasis on the requirements for ordinary infallibility, but with the same affirmative results in regards to the teaching on the patriarchal hierarchy of the family: "It must be clear that they are teaching it *definitively*, as something which *must* be held. Therefore, one must ascertain 1) what exactly is being taught; 2) whether the Pope and bishops are all teaching it [i.e. moral unanimity]; and 3) what degree of certitude they are attaching to their teaching."[34]

In regards to the Catechism of Trent, the first two requirements are fulfilled: it is clear what is being taught, and it is being taught in a definitive manner. The third requirement also appears to be fulfilled due to the wording of the Catechism of Trent's teaching: "Again, and in this the conjugal union *chiefly* consists, let wives *never* forget that next to God they are to love their husbands, to esteem them above all others, yielding to

---

33. *Codex Juris Canonici* (1917), Canon 227. This definition is from the Code of Canon Law that was in force from 1917-1983. The new Code's reference is much briefer.

34. James T. O'Connor, *The Gift of Infallibility* (Boston, Daughters of St. Paul, 1986), p. 106.

them in all things not inconsistent to Christian piety, a willing and ready obedience." *(Emphasis* mine)

The consistent exegesis of Ephesians 5 and the numerous reiteration of the Popes that teach patriarchal hierarchy as a Catholic moral imperative also appear to fulfill the requirements for ordinary infallibility. In his landmark encyclical on Christian marriage, *Casti Connubii,* Pope Pius XI specifically characterizes the teaching on patriarchal hierarchy as an unchangeable law of God: "This order [i.e. "the primacy of the husband over his wife and children, and the ready submission and willing obedience of the wife"[35]] was constituted by an authority higher than man's, that is, by the authority and wisdom of God Himself, and neither the laws of the State nor the good pleasure of individuals can ever change it."[36] Such an authoritative statement in a papal encyclical addressed to all the Bishops of the world lacks neither clarity, nor definition, nor certitude, nor universality.

The Harmony of Hierarchy

Sin is the source of all chaos, for it is a rebellion against God's established order. As such sin is the cause of familial discord. Harmony is defined by St. Thomas Aquinas as "an effect of charity, which does not necessarily imply unity of opinion, but of wills." Hence familial harmony depends not on unity of opinion—often a rare and tenuous commodity between man and woman—but upon a unity of wills. This unity of wills and the ensuing harmony can only be complete in a hierarchical order, which fosters a harmony and openness between man and wife that is made possible by the absence of infighting and power struggles. Since the familial hierarchical structure does

---

35. Pope Pius XI, *Casti Connubii,* December 31, 1930; para. 26.
36. *Ibid.;* para. 77.

not admit of politics or consensus opinion, the man as head of the family is not threatened by his wife's input, or creativity, or difference of opinion; indeed he welcomes these things, because his authority is irrevocably established. And the wife need not be unbecomingly aggressive in a ceaseless struggle for power, but rather may employ her unique feminine qualities to influence and strengthen her husband in his decision-making.

In a time when the family must be united as never before, it is the harmony of hierarchy that unites the family as nothing else can. In referring to St. Paul's delineation of the relationship of Christ and the Church as it applies to man and wife, Pope Pius XII again provides insight into the blessings of the hierarchical order:

He has shown how firm command and respectful, docile obedience can and should find forgetfulness of self and a generous, reciprocal giving in active and mutual love. From these sentiments, then, let there spring and grow that domestic peace, the fruit of order and affection, which St. Augustine defines as: *ordinata imperandi obediendique concordia cohabitantium* (the harmonious union of authority and obedience among those who live together). This must be the ideal of your Christian family.[37]

---

37. Pius XII, Allocution to Newly-weds.

CHAPTER 3

The Principles of Authentic Christian Patriarchy

IN THESE DAYS of both hyper-egalitarianism and hyper-nationalism,[1] there are some ardent Catholics who would like to bring back the rule of the ancient hereditary monarchies. However, as pure as this intent may be, there are but two monarchies established for all time by divine ordinance: that of the Catholic Church and that of the Catholic family.[2] These dual monarchies are, respectively, sacerdotal and paternal; as such, they are patriarchal. It is in this sense that all Catholics are necessarily monarchists and, more specifically, patriarchists. It is crucial then—and all the more urgent in these days of ecclesiastical

---

1. Nationalism here refers to the movement toward artificial state conglomerations of regional peoples and ethnicities, be these conglomerations the established individual nation states or the hyper- and supra-nationalism of unified nations. It is individual state nationalism that has made possible multi-state nationalism. Nationalism moves away from subsidiarity and communal individuation by stressing what people have in common at the lowest denominator at the expense of their inherent and vital differences.

2. Though there is a natural propriety for male headship, even fundamentalist Protestants, who stress the patriarchal headship of the family, have no *extraordinary* divine commission for their authority since they themselves reject the divine commission of the Church and may reject the very sacramentality of marriage. Though there was an effort to support familial patriarchy at the start of the Protestant movement (an effort still present in certain fundamentalist sects) it was doomed from the beginning due to Protestantism's defining rejection of the ecclesiastical patriarchy, a rejection that began with the papacy, but soon included the episcopacy and the priesthood. A "protesting" patriarch, or a patriarchy under no absolute, given tangible authority, is a loose cannon indeed. Similar seeds of destruction can be seen in the official rejection by many Protestant sects of the sacramentality of marriage and the resultant allowance of divorce and later admittance of contraception.

and familial emasculation—to seek the revivification of these two God-ordained monarchies.

Before examining the character of the Catholic patriarch, a brief prelude is required. Regardless of how ranging and otherwise incongruous a person's other positions of belief, the acceptance of the hierarchical structure of the Church's Magisterium remains the *sine qua non* for all who would claim to be orthodox Catholics. But this is not so with the other God-ordained hierarchical structure. Indeed, unlike ecclesiastical patriarchy, which is the lowest common denominator of Catholic orthodoxy,[3] familial patriarchy is the most divisive of orthodox concepts. For there is nothing that so contradicts the contemporary ethos of equality at all costs, or impedes the omnipotent rule of the modern state than that of the patriarchal hierarchy of the family: the teaching that prescribes a man's spiritual and juridical headship over his wife and children.

Nonetheless familial hierarchy, like ecclesiastical hierarchy, is a constant teaching of the Church. From first-century epistles to twentieth-century encyclicals, it has been proclaimed and affirmed. The Catechism of Trent, whose universal episcopal acceptance and promulgation guarantees its dogmatic and moral teachings,[4] has this to say about the duties of a wife: "Again, and in this the conjugal union *chiefly* consists, let wives never forget that next to God they are to love their husbands, to esteem them above all others, yielding to them in all things not inconsistent with Christian piety, a willing and ready

---

3. The acceptance of the Catholic ecclesiastical patriarchy, or the Catholic Magisterium, is what formally makes one a Catholic. For this acceptance entails the acceptance of the entire Christian faith, as opposed to separate articles, no matter how fundamental—such as those of a Christological nature.

4. In proposing a teaching of faith or morals as one to be held by all the faithful, the totality of the bishops in union with the Pope exercise infallibility both in an *extraordinary manner*, when they are assembled in a general council, and in an *ordinary manner*, when scattered over the earth.

obedience" (emphasis mine). There has never been a worldly plenipotentiary that could claim such allegiance.

However, the true nature and charism of Christian patriarchy/leadership differs radically from that of a worldly sort. This chapter deals with the essential characteristic difference in those that are commissioned to be Catholic leaders: be they churchmen or family men.

The Essential Paradox

Historically, much of Christian leadership has been built upon and intermeshed with secular leadership. Still, though it has not always been adequately recognized, these two modes of leadership have a radical essential difference, for to rule in the Christian order always entails a paradox not present in the secular understanding.

Our Lord Jesus Christ pointed out the difference between His and the world's understanding of authority in response to the apostles' vying for positions of honor.

> And Jesus called them to him and said to them, "You know that they who seem to rule over the Gentiles, lord it over them: and their princes have power over them. But it is not so among you: but whosoever will be greater, shall be your minister. And whosoever will be first among you, shall be the servant of all."[5]

The ultimate paradigm of the Christian ruler is Christ: He who paradoxically combines both king and suffering servant. The paradox of Christian leadership derives from the paradox of the Redemption, where Christ the King, the Master of the Universe, emptied and immolated Himself at the hands of His

---

5. Mark 10:42-44 .

subjects and for His subjects. It is Christ-like sacrificial head-ship, then, that is the specific difference of Catholic patriarchy: be it found in familial patriarchs who are called to love their wives "as Christ also loved the church, and delivered himself up for it,"[6] or in ecclesiastical patriarchs, priests, and bishops, who are called to replicate exactly this love of Christ for His Church.

The Paradox of Manly Magnanimity

In addition to the paradox of the ruler who is simultaneously suffering servant, there is the paradox that allows the Catholic patriarch to be strong and uncompromising in the service of God, and noble in comportment and bearing as befitting his office, yet, at the same time, humble and meek. The virtue that makes this possible is magnanimity (Lat. *magnus*, great; *animus*, spirit). Josef Pieper, in a redaction of St. Thomas, explains mag-nanimity in this way:

> Magnanimity is the expansion of the spirit toward great things; one who expects great things of himself and makes himself worthy of it is magnanimous. The magnanimous man is to a certain extent "particular": he does not allow himself to become concerned with everything that comes along, but rather only with those great things that are suit-able for him. Magnanimity seeks above all great glory: "The magnanimous man strives toward that which is worthy of the highest glory." In the *Summa Theologica* it is stated, "If one disdains glory in such a manner that he makes no effort to do that which merits glory, that action is blameworthy" ... Undaunted uprightness is the distinctive mark of mag-nanimity, while nothing is more alien to it than this: to be

---

6. Eph. 5:25.

silent out of fear for what is true. One who is magnanimous completely shuns flattery and hypocrisy, both of which are the issue of a mean heart. The magnanimous man does not complain, for his heart does not permit him to be overcome by any external evil. Magnanimity encompasses an unshakable firmness of hope, a plainly defiant certainty, and the thorough calm of a fearless heart. The magnanimous man submits himself not to the confusion of feelings or to any human being or to fate—but only to God.[7]

In a Christian sense, magnanimity is a greatness of spirit that is derived not from a man's estimation of his person, by rather from his confidence and esteem of God, and subsequently of his Faith, his family, his patriarchal office, and his dedication to these great causes. Such a man bears himself in a manner suited for the nobility of his office and cause. The magnanimous man's noble bearing demands that others treat him accordingly. But he does not derive his nobility from human respect, rather from a cause espoused. As such, he is undiminished by those who fail to render an appropriate respect.

An authentic magnanimity does not admit of the charges of chauvinism that are so shrilly bantered about in this age of hyper-egalitarianism, nor is it proscribed by the Christian teaching on the virtue of humility and the vice of pride. The glory that the truly magnanimous man seeks is not his own but God's: *Ad Majorem Dei Gloriam.* Insofar as the magnanimous man recognizes God's glory, he recognizes his own wretchedness when apart from God. In seeking glory, the magnanimous man would ascribe to this ancient Spanish Catholic familial motto: *To lose one's life for one's honor, to lose one's honor for one's soul.* He does the right thing for Faith, family, and homeland, even

---

7. J. Pieper, *A Brief Reader on the Virtues of the Human Heart* (San Francisco, Ignatius Press, 1991), pp. 37-39.

when that right thing means physical death or, worse yet, the death of his reputation.

Every son of Adam is affected by concupiscence, by inordinate self-love and pride. However, the base man serves his self-love and pride by serving his body and emotions, by seeking pleasure and avoiding pain; whereas the noble man serves his self-love and pride by subordinating his bodily desires and emotions in service of an ideal or cause, by forgoing pleasure and embracing pain. The noble man idealizes his self-love and pride, makes it bigger than himself, as is befitting a spiritual being. In doing so, he intellectualizes and codifies that self-love and pride, as it were, brings it out in the open and lays it on the line where it can be tested, thus making it vulnerable. And such is the limit of magnanimity for the pagan, with the best fruit that comes from the combination of the magnanimous pagan's idealism and vulnerability being Stoicism.

However, for the magnanimous Christian, this self-love and pride, which is no longer a love of creature comforts but of honor—be it name, family, or cause—can become totally transformed into love and esteem for God if one accepts the action of vulnerability which is the purgation of humiliation. Humiliation is clear cut and searing for the honorable Christian man: for only he who seeks perfection with his whole being can feel the full effect of his utter inability and failure to be perfect.

The magnanimous pagan, without the sanctification of suffering and the beatitude of communion with God, cannot bear to enter into the full depths of humiliation. Thus, he steels himself against feeling the full effects of the vicissitudes of life or, when this no longer suffices, may take that very life. However, the magnanimous Christian is able to enter fully into his humiliation, even be thankful for it, as he turns with an all-consuming passion from himself and his wretchedness to the glory and perfection of God. Thus, for the Christian, magnanimity is a precursor to holiness, and holiness the fulfillment and only sure guarantee for magnanimity.

It was magnanimity in union with humility that G.K. Chesterton implicated when he spoke of St. Thomas Becket, who "wore a hair shirt under his gold and crimson, and there is much to be said of the combination; for Becket got the benefit of the hair shirt while the people in the street got the benefit of the crimson and gold."

Or in the same section of *Orthodoxy,* when Chesterton stated that the Christian challenge was not, "Neither swagger nor grovel," but rather, "Here you can swagger and there you can grovel." Or, again, when he spoke of the soul of the great Christian King St. Louis who personified the scriptural prophecy of the lion lying down with the lamb, which is not to be mistaken for "that when the lion lies down with the lamb the lion becomes lamb-like. That is simply the lamb absorbing the lion instead of the lion eating the lamb. The real problem is—can the lion lie down with the lamb and still retain his royal ferocity?"[8]

Chesterton could have just as well asked, "Can magnanimity lie down with humility: can the great-spirited man, the militant Christian patriarch, be at one and the same time the meek and humble man?" And, of course, the answer is a resounding "yes" as made manifest in the phenomenon of a king-saint. For humility is the honest appraisal of oneself, both in its recognition of one's total dependence on God, and in its recognition of the gifts and commissions that God has bestowed upon oneself.

It is the magnanimous man who confidently prays with the psalmist at the opening of Holy Mass: "*Judica me, Deus, et discerne*

---

8. G.K. Chesterton, *Orthodoxy* (New York, Dodd, Mead and Company, 1957), pp. 180-182.

causam meam de gente non sancta: ab homine iniquo et doloso erue me."[9]
It is the magnanimous man who is staunchly recusant in his
refusal to submit to the authority of a schismatic church in
England, or an atheistic state in Russia, or an immoral law in
secular America. It is the magnanimous man who in his patriarchal office boldly defends and advances the cause of Faith and
family, regardless of the odds, regardless of the cost, regardless
of public opinion. Magnanimity could be said to be a militant
exultation in God: in His Church, in His cause, and in one's
service of Him.

Magnanimity depends both on the greatness of a man's con-
cerns, which he can choose and develop, and upon his natural
baseline aptitude. Nevertheless, as grace builds upon nature,
every Christian has an essential magnanimity of spirit that
derives from the great cause of bringing about the Kingdom
and the striving for eternal glory—a glory for which his soul
received the capacity through Baptism. Hence, no matter how
limited one may be in his aptitude, the individual Christian cannot be said to be incapable of "greatness of spirit," due to the
common Christian vocation. St. Thérèse of Lisieux compared
individuals to cups, which though varying in capacity (magni-
tude), are nonetheless all full when filled to the brim. Hence
a full thimble is more perfect than a half-full tumbler. In this
manner a man with less natural aptitude that has fulfilled or
perfected his potential in Christ can be deemed greater than a
man with greater aptitude that has only half-fulfilled his potential; for the perfect man is greater in the Kingdom of God than
the less perfect.

---

9. "Judge me, O God, and distinguish my cause from the nation that is not holy;
   deliver me from the unjust and deceitful man."

The Great Cause

To be a magnanimous man one must espouse a great cause, and to espouse a great cause one must have a great faith. There is no greater cause or faith than the Catholic Faith, hence the Catholic man is called to be the most magnanimous of all. No system of thought ever came close to formulating, much less upholding, ideals as high as those of the Catholic Church. No cause ever issued a challenge that can begin to compare to the Church's call to heroic greatness. No organization has ever come close to producing the steady stream of heroes that have been produced by the Catholic Church in her 2,000-year existence.

To espouse a great cause means to make it one's own, that is, to have a passionate vision of the heroic and personal waging of that cause. Such an espoused cause will animate all a man's actions, for it is the motivation and final end of those actions. Some men may be convinced in theory of the rightness of something, but remain unpersuaded in implementation. But the magnanimous man is not only intellectually convinced of the truth of his cause, but engraves this truth deeply in his heart and is morally persuaded to live it out. The magnanimous man holds his noble cause so deeply in fact, that it becomes one with him, inseparable from who he is.

But it takes great effort to wed a cause and to develop a subsequent vision, especially for men who are used to entering into easy emotional "causes" such as sporting events or movie dramas. For the development of a vision requires a deep personal and sacrificial commitment to one's cause. This requisite passion is not to be equated with emotionalism but rather with that passion of self-sacrificial love, that passion of self-abnegation, that passion from whence Christ's final hour takes its name.

"Passion is conducive to genius"; so said the great man of

Catholic letters, Hilaire Belloc. It is while in the throes of a life-long passionate commitment to a great cause that the grandest vision a man is capable of envisioning will be produced, and it is the promulgation of the vision that raises him to his full moral and spiritual stature. Yes, such a passion is all consuming and apt to be labeled "fanatical." But fanaticism is based on emotion rather than deep intellectual conviction and sacrificial love. Fanatical is he who is disproportionately devoted to something irrational or unworthy of his rendered enthusiasm. The sports fan(atic) represents the perfect example. For a sporting event to be really enjoyable, the spectator must imbue it with meaning; the more meaning he gives it the bigger and more exciting the game. But no self-sacrifice is involved for the spectator. And no matter how much importance one gives a game it remains just that, a game. As such, it can never be a worthy recipient of a man's passionate devotion.

For the Catholic, the cause of the Faith necessarily entails the cause of the family, that is, the domestic church. Indeed, together Faith and Family form one cause, and both entail all facets of human existence in so far as these facets either impede or facilitate the bringing about of the Kingdom and personal sanctification. It is finally only the cause of the Faith and family that is fully worthy of a Catholic man's total devotion, and from which all other worthy causes—from the patriotic[10] to the practical, from the idealistic to investigative—derive their worth.

This great twofold cause of Faith and family is the bringing about of Christ's kingdom by advancing His truth and the Holy Church Militant, and by advancing personal, familial, and

---

10. It is, most obviously, that from the cause of Faith and family *all* true and just Catholic patriotic and political causes flow. Even for non-Catholics and in the realm of secular politics the good of the family, which is the basic and prerequisite unit of society, properly remains the touchstone of patriotism and politics.

communal holiness. If the father of the family or the priest of a parish claims that he wants his family members or parishioners to be saints—and to bring them to sanctity is the summation of his duties to them—then he himself must be heroically engaged in bringing about the Kingdom; for cowards or slackers are not the fathers of martyrs, and only those made of the stuff of martyrs will be the saints of an ominous tomorrow.

The Basis of Patriarchal Authority

Ultimately, then, a Christian patriarch's greatness of spirit, his magnanimity, derives from Christ and espousing the bringing about of His Kingdom. So too, a Christian patriarch's headship, his authority, derives from Christ and His divine commission. Once in line and imbued with Christ's authority, patriarchy no longer depends on a man's natural, and quite contingent, ability to subjugate and dominate, or even provide and protect (though this is intrinsic to the duty of patriarchy) by means of physical, mental, or financial prowess. Rather this patriarchal authority is based upon an enduring spiritual commission. Whereas in the ancient past men ruled the family and clan by a patriarchy of force and power or, as civilization developed, by means of cultural decree, in the Christian dispensation they rule by means of a spiritual commission that derives its authority from Christ, and its efficacy from a man's conforming of himself to Christ. And such a spiritual patriarchy is much more absolute and enduring than any mere patriarchy of brute force or cultural structure.

As such, Catholic patriarchal authority, be it familial or ecclesiastical, is not based on any temporal status, nor swayed by any temporal vicissitude, but rather established permanently and solely on Christ and His commission. No longer does society or the state back up the Church's or the father's authority;

indeed they are placed at odds. As such, Catholic patriarchal authority can be seen clearly for what it is: a purely moral mandate. And a moral mandate is the highest of mandates because it calls for a fully human response; a response that entails the use of reason and free will, that is, the rational assent to truth and the volitional embracing of the good. As a moral mandate then, Catholic patriarchal authority calls for a submission that is absolute: a submission that is *to* truth and *of* love. (And here let it suffice to say that the world's pejorative and negative understanding of "submission," with its connotations of mere passivity as opposed to fecund receptivity—the very type of submissive receptivity that is involved in *any* person's sanctification—is as far from the proper Christian understanding as is its pejorative understanding of "patriarchy," which has been herein elucidated upon.)

While the Catholic patriarchal office—be it ecclesiastical or familial—mandates by the authority of Christ an absolute submission on the part of those under its charge, it also mandates that its officeholder absolutely loves those with whom he is charged. In accord with a sacred *noblesse oblige*, this patriarchal responsibility to love must accord with its source of privilege and authority, which is Christ. Thus it entails loving as Christ loved: with an absolute, sacrificial love. So as Catholic patriarchal authority mandates a submission from its subjects unlike any other, because it is not based on temporal power or brute strength but rather on the immutable commission of Christ, it likewise demands more from the patriarch than is expected from any worldly leader because it demands all, the very giving of one's life.

The Catholic patriarch spurns the rule of power and self-interest that characterizes the world's understanding of authority, and instead follows the example of Christ, from whom he derives his authority. And how was it that Christ led? He was wrathfully militant when piety and His Father's house were besmirched, but gentle and compassionate to the contrite sinner. He spoke forcefully and courageously in promulgation of the truth, but was silent and long-suffering at the time of His trial. His teachings on the way of holiness and the need for self-abnegation where clear and uncompromising, but His personal example of embracing the Cross was His final, most eloquent sermon ever. And He loved unto the laying down of his life for those that were given to Him. It is in this divine manner that the Catholic patriarch must strive to fulfill his great God-given commission.

For the Christian patriarch this Cross, which is the very trademark of the Catholic Faith, entails within it both the Scepter and the Crosier. It is the Cross that when melded with the Scepter of kingly authority makes that authority Christlike. It is the Cross that when melded with the Crosier of teaching and spiritual guidance makes that teaching authentic and guidance prophetic. And it is in the embracing of this triune staff—this melded Scepter/Crosier/Cross—that causes the Christian patriarch first and most vigorously to hold the Scepter of Christ's kingly authority over his own unruly passions and pride; and first and most obediently to submit his intellect and will to the Crosier of Christ's teachings and personal beckoning; and first and most pentitentially to pick up the Cross of Christ and unite himself to it in his own salvific crucifixion.

Embracing these three marks of manhood, brandishing this triune staff of Scepter, Crosier, and Cross, arms the Christian patriarch with the tools of his vocation, enabling him to serve his family as holy priest, courageous prophet, and loving king.

CHAPTER 4

The Scepter of Self-Discipline

THE SCEPTER OF AUTHORITY over oneself, or the Scepter of Self-Discipline, is the perquisite of Christian patriarchy. Indeed, it is the prerequisite for authentic conversion as well. Repent, turn from your sins. It is only after a man has turned firmly from his sins, that is, became habituated in his turn from mortal sin, that he can further wield the triune staff.

Many a young man has momentarily experienced the strange, self-conscious realization that he is now full grown, a man standing in the place of his father. Maybe it occurs to him as he is shaving and he flashes back to the time when he watched with awe as his father, so strong and sure, undertook this daily ritual of manhood. Or maybe it occurs to him as he looks into the upturned face of his child, whose eyes are now filled with the unlimited trust and confidence that he once bestowed upon his own father.

The nostalgia of this strange self-consciousness is often accompanied by a feeling of inadequacy. And understandably so, for the office of manhood is such that it will always require a man to reach beyond himself as he strives to fulfill its high office worthily. This uneasiness or strangeness in holding the office of fatherhood transcends all times and places; but feelings of inadequacy, even of alienation, in regard to one's manhood, are especially prevalent in the present age, when at the time of a boy's adolescence there is no process of initiation into the ranks of manhood.

Adolescence is by definition the period of gender

actualization. To coincide with the boy's physical maturation, communities and cultures have traditionally called him to manhood, either through some formal initiation that requires him to demonstrate certain virtues of manhood, or through the bestowing of a new adult status, where again he is expected to demonstrate to the family and the community the traits of manhood. In either case, a boy gained both a new respect from the community and added communal responsibilities. In his new status he was expected to strive for and live up to a defined ideal of manhood. But today, in the West, this is not the case; rather adolescence is viewed as a time that offers many of the privileges and freedoms of the adult, but few of the responsibilities. Adolescence (including the collegiate years) is now the time to have fun, the last hurrah before the drudgery of adulthood sets in. An idyllic belief that adolescence is the best time of life is perpetuated by adults who harbor regrets that they didn't live their own youth to its fullest, or secretly wish they could go back, and somehow vicariously seek to live it again through their children.

It is during adolescence that habits and values are most readily inculcated, for the child enters adolescence with his character at its most impressionable. In early adolescence the character is still in flux, yet will become increasingly consistent with maturation and thus apt to retaining impressions. As a young adult emerges from adolescence his character gains a solidity that renders it resistant to remolding. More often than not, the habits and values developed during adolescence are carried over and enshrined for a lifetime (which may account for why many adults idealize adolescence). This adult retention of the values and spirit of adolescence is apparent in the West's popular culture which, at best, can be characterized as "juvenile." One need only observe the tenor and style of the various presentations and campaigns of the entertainment and advertising industries, whose success depends on its mass appeal, to realize that extended adolescence is endemic to our culture.

If a Christian community is desirous of a future adult population that will be committed to and inculcated with the values of the Faith and the family (for example, the roles of fatherhood and motherhood) then they must conclude the inculcation of those values during adolescence. Thus the formal call to manhood is properly issued at the onset of this formative period. During adolescence the scepter of authority is to be emphasized. But the subject of this authority is over the boy himself rather than others; for before he wields the scepter of authority over others he must wield the scepter of authority over himself, thus developing an interior moral authority and the virtues requisite of manhood. This scepter of authority wielded over oneself is more succinctly *the scepter of self-discipline*. Once the young man has acquired the self-discipline and virtues of manhood he will be able to exercise his authority justly and sure-handedly over those eventually given over to his charge.

The Romance of Manhood

Early adolescence is the time of idealism and limitless dreams. For it is the time of transformation and growth, and growth requires that "a man's reach should exceed his grasp," as Robert Browning put it. Dreams and ideals are the Lord's way of beckoning and inspiring a boy to leave his childhood and venture into the realm of manhood, into the realm of greatness and sanctity. Fostering and directing this idealism is the overall goal of adolescent formation.

Boys naturally enough imagine themselves in situations that test and demonstrate their manhood. In the past, military exploits often provided the usual genre for these dreams; today it is predominately sports. But whereas military valor may be the epitome of secular virtue (and in the service of a noble cause is indeed worthy of admiration and emulation) athletics must remain intrinsically but *the playing of games*: an important means to an end, but finally unworthy of a boy's highest dreams and aspirations. Sports[11] are beneficial for the adolescent in that they provide a real testing ground for his emerging manhood, but they are to be played, not idealized.

Yet in today's entertainment-crazed culture, sports are viewed as the ultimate expression of manhood, rather than as the training exercise they properly are. Promoting sports as a tool of formation—where games of physical prowess are ordered toward the real battles of life and the development of moral and spiritual prowess—is drastically different than treating them as ends in themselves. When the summation of a boy's dreams is to play professional sports, he is selling himself short of a greatness that far exceeds the playing of games, or, for that matter, the making of money. Sports must be seen in a proper perspective, a perspective that values them as a preparation for, but still a pale reflection of, the real drama of life: the absolute battle between good and evil that is fought in every soul and that is waged collectively by the Church Militant.

It is the romance of Christian manhood itself that should form the basis of a boy's idealism; that is, his dreams should be of the fulfillment of his manhood. It is at this time that he begins to discern that first outline of his vision, of what sort of

---

11. Young men are also formed, and arguably formed better, when they engage in "natural" activities such as encountering wildlife, climbing trees, rocks, and mountains, hiking, hunting, fishing, trapping, and farming or subsistence gardening. These activities are all conducive to self-sufficiency, and are not subject to the egocentricity of organized sports, but rather acquaint the boy with real life and natural law, thus simultaneously humbling and strengthening the character and psyche. Unlike the artificial and perfect playing field of sports, these natural activities not only reflect reality but are reality.

man he desires to be. The vision will vary depending on vocational or aptitudinal differences, will be of a greater or lesser magnanimity depending on the soul of the boy, but will, nonetheless, share the magnanimity of the universal call to Christian manhood. For it is the vocation of fatherhood, which in itself requires "greatness of soul," that fulfills manhood regardless of the state of life—be it lay, religious, or priestly—the young man eventually pursues.

All of a young man's powers and faculties are marshaled, unified, and made tangible when he embraces and dedicates himself to a cause. And it is the greatness of the cause that evokes greatness of soul. The fundamental cause—indeed the greatest and only absolute cause—to be embraced by a Catholic young man is the cause of Christ and His Church. During adolescence a boy is most propitiously disposed to espouse the cause of Christ, for it is a time when his spiritual sensitivity is heightened, and his thoughts take a more introspective and profound turn. Under the right influences he becomes increasingly attuned to the promptings of the Holy Spirit. It is at this time that a youth will receive his first intimations of a vocation to the religious life or priesthood. But regardless of his eventual state of life, he is now called to choose between "the two standards," as St. Ignatius describes in his *Spiritual Exercises*.[12] A fundamental cause requires a fundamental choice: the standard of the world, the Evil One and his minions, or the standard of Christ and His Church Militant. Such a choice is necessary for the boy to begin his odyssey of manhood. The cause of Christ is an all-inclusive one, marshaling all the virtues of manhood in its service. It is a cause that calls the young man to sanctity, a sanctity that is nothing more than the perfection of his Christian manhood. Holiness *equals* manhood: this is the equation that must become engraved on the young man's heart.

---

12. St. Ignatius of Loyola, *The Spiritual Exercises*, Week II, Day IV.

The Scepter of Self-Discipline

Once a young man has chosen to serve under the standard of Christ and His Church—and again this is the fundamental choice and subsequent orientation of his manhood—then he may begin the task of identifying and acquiring the virtues of manhood. Such a task requires the wielding of the staff of self-discipline; for though it is necessary to present the ideals of manhood to the boy, and indeed challenge and encourage him in his pursuit of these ideals, it is only the boy himself that can embrace them.

Adolescence is the most intensive and potentially profitable period of growth in a man's life. It is a time of physical transformation, growth, and surging emotions that is properly paralleled by the development of the boy's moral powers of self-governance. While physiological maturation results in the emergence of the secondary sexual characteristics of masculinity, moral growth entails the development of the virtues of manhood. The boy's increase in physical virility and the accompanying emotions produce a powerful raw force that requires a corresponding increase in moral strength that will enable him to harness, discipline, and direct this newly emergent virility.

The time of adolescence, then, is a time of discipline, and specifically manly discipline. This manly discipline, however, is not so much imposed from without as fostered from within. In order for the boy to mature morally and spiritually he must begin to internalize and make his own the values and ideals of both the Faith and his family. Those in charge of his formation, the father foremost, must adopt an attitude that views the youth *as an apprentice and initiate to manhood.* As such, the key pedagogical principle is to treat the youngster like a man and expect him to act like a man. And *when* (not *if*) he fails to act like a man, he is subsequently deprived, to a degree proportional to his offense, of the honor of being treated like a man. But since punishment is necessarily coercive and does directly entail the principle of self-discipline, it is to be used always within the overall context of promoting the goal of self-discipline and not as a primary means of adolescent formation.

The Father is the Main Mentor

At the time of adolescence it is the father who should become the primary influence in his boy's life. The father, by example and word, must challenge his son to manhood. He must begin to look upon his son as a man, and, as such, expect him to act like a man. While understanding that his son is still in the process of becoming a man, the father must, nonetheless, expect his son, in no uncertain terms, to embrace and strive for, both intellectually and morally, the ideals of manhood, and in so doing form the foundation for the lifelong process of perfecting his manhood. The father should be the primary source of encouragement to his son, viewing him as one who is joining the ranks, flesh of his flesh who will carry on the battle after him. It is time for the father to become a mentor to his son, to convey the cause and the vision of his own manhood, and seek to discern and nourish those of his son. The father must, therefore, have a cause and a vision that he has made his own, and seek to live it out wholeheartedly; for this is a time of heart-to-heart, father to son, man-to-man talks, where only integrity suffices. Today, due to deficient formation in his own adolescence, many a father will lack such a cause and a vision, and therefore have to undergo his own remedial formation in adulthood.

Developing a Man-to-Man Relationship

Integrity, honesty, frankness—all aspects of truthfulness—
must be upheld and practiced by both father and son. For honesty concerning oneself is the prerequisite to moral growth;
one must recognize one's deficiencies before one can begin to
rectify them. And thus *frankness* is the specific character of a
man-to-man relationship that goes beyond the superficiality
of sociability and forms the bonds of true brotherhood. The
development of a man-to-man relationship between a father
and son entails acquiring a deeper understanding of each other
as men, that is, as individuals, rather than as the other half of
the father/son relationship. This does not mean that the relationship of father to son is diminished, but, on the contrary, it
is to deepen and mature. The adolescent must begin to realize
that his father is a mere mortal, rather than the omnipotent,
omniscient figure of childhood. A father should not try to fore-
stall that realization by exerting an overly formal or aloof bearing. But neither should that realization detract from the father's
position of authority; instead it should serve to reinforce his
authority by grounding it in the divine commission of Christ
rather than in the human competency of the father. Hence, the
newly recognized humanity of the father is a teaching moment
in which the meaning of the office of manhood and fatherhood
can be conveyed.

The father in turn begins to see his son as a young man who
will soon share his lot in life, his patriarchal commission. Father
and son, then, should bond in mutual sympathy as they seek
to fulfill their common commission to serve and stand in the
stead of God the Father. The development of this man-to-man
relationship may also require the severing of a mother's apron
strings. For such maternal ribbons, leading as they do back to a
sanctuary where the call of manhood is mercifully muted, may

tempt the boy to retreat from the steep road of manly self-sufficiency that he must travel.

Not a Time for the Feminine

Contrary to popular belief, adolescence is not a time for the boy to be immersed in, preoccupied with, or ordered toward, the feminine. Rather he should be concerned with the masculine and the acquisition of its traits. Of course as a boy's virility waxes so does his interest in the opposite sex. But this newly emergent virility is properly channeled toward the boy's acquirement of manhood and its accompanying strengths, which enables this virility to become a powerful catalyst for growth in all facets of his life. Without the challenges of manhood being presented to him—and first and foremost the moral and spiritual challenges of manly chastity—he will become dissipate and squanderous of his virility. There is a time and a place for the energies of a young man to be turned to the wooing of a future wife, but adolescence is not that time. Instead, adolescence is the time of discipline and growth, when the boy conforms himself to the ideals of manhood.

Before a man is ready to take upon himself the responsibilities of marriage and family, or other forms of patriarchal authority, he must first be inculcated with the character of manhood. In today's world, men too often seek their masculine identity in a relationship with a woman. They seek to please their girlfriend (or fiancée) by being the man she wants them to be. In wooing the desired young lady, the suitor seeks to affirm his own worth, or desirability as a man. Many a man today enters into marriage still seeking the definition of who he is as a man. When a young man enters into the marriage before he has realized his manhood, his identity as a man is likely to become dependent upon his wife's affirmation. But since a woman can never experience the initiation into the ranks of manhood, she is incapable of leading a man into it. Though a good wife may facilitate her husband's manhood, she is unable to bestow it. Initiation comes from either the formal trials administered by previous initiates to manhood, or the random vicissitudes of a young man's own search for manhood.

No matter how the entry into manhood is accomplished— be it formally and at a specific time or informally and over a period of time—it is always deeply personal. Peers, clubs, and superiors can only lead the initiate up to the threshold; from then on out it is a solitary, personal process. Finally the entry into manhood must be accomplished alone; alone, that is, save the presence of Christ, who in the deepest recesses of the initiate's heart is the anchor of masculine identity and manhood. Such a man, in essence, is capable of standing alone in the world or standing up to the world with Christ as its sole support: he has a certain rugged individualism or, more aptly, autonomy in Christ. Only when a man has achieved such a masculine identity will he be able to stand as the head of others and in God's stead as a Christian patriarch.

Brotherhood and Schools of Initiation

Still, the blessings of true friends along the way are priceless indeed. Although a father (or a father figure) is crucial for the boy as he enters early manhood, brotherhood is most beneficial. And here a father cannot take upon himself the role of brother without crossing the line that demarcates the authority and dignity of his fatherhood. For the peers of early manhood test and measure their strength and character against one another; they challenge one another, taunt and butt heads with one another. In doing so they form a brotherly bond of mutual edification and respect.

"Peer pressure" has become a pejorative today, and yet it is a desirable, even necessary element in a boy's growth. Aristotle considers true friendship only possible among men "who are similar in virtue."[13] For the Catholic man, true friends share not only virtue, but Christ, and a common vision of the Faith. Such is the dynamic of positive Catholic peer pressure: young men united together in the common cause of the Faith as they strive to develop the strengths of Catholic manhood.

Yet once more the present day does not afford the requisite atmosphere for manly development. Brotherhood is now nearly extinct in our society as men seek manly affirmation from women and interact with each other only on the most superficial levels. Men play or watch games together, or pursue some other adolescent enjoyment; they rarely converse as men, solemnly, and in consideration of important issues, and rarely join together in a common cause of a noble and grave nature.

The acquisition of brothers in Christ is one reason that it is desirable to seek out a Catholic boy's preparatory school of initiation; the other is its pedagogical function. When a boy's preparatory school is based upon the pedagogy of initiation, and works in close conjunction and harmony with the father, the task of ushering the boy into manhood is greatly facilitated. In such a school a certain objectivity and formality in standards and performance evaluation is present, to a degree not suitable to the home or to the father/son relationship. The atmosphere of the school as compared to the home is somewhat harsh, for fatherly love (not to mention motherly love) is absent. Though a schoolmaster may look upon his boys in much the same way as the father looks upon his son, a schoolmaster's tolerance is necessarily limited; and his standards, understandably, must be more objective since they deal with a composite group of

---

13. Aristotle, *Nicomachean Ethics*, Book 8, 1159b.

boys. A father's love for his son requires that he never give up on his boy; whereas, a schoolmaster's duty requires that he set limits of tolerance for the benefit of the entire student body.

There is a natural subculture that develops among all boys who develop friendships and bond as brothers. It is a necessary part of their development as self-sufficient men. It is clandestine because it is intimate, and it is intimate because it involves the tenuous affirmation of one another's manhood. But this subculture need not be in its ideals opposed to those ideals of the school. Rather when the school, in conjunction with the students' fathers, upholds the essential ideals and virtues of Catholic manhood; when it sets a challenging standard that demands the boy shape up or ship out; when it views, as does the student's father, the boy as a future comrade in arms; when integrity is manifest and the ideals are the same for one and all; when the students are challenged to embrace the Faith as men; when self-discipline is the object of all correction; then peer groups will form a subculture that in Christian principle parallels that of the familial and academic establishment. But today, again due to today's great dearth of Catholic men and fathers, such institutions are sadly lacking.

The school and the home must work in conjunction in advancing not only the boy's academic growth, but his moral growth as well. Where the school implements its standards of conduct in an impersonal manner, the home implements it in a personal manner. In either case, the key to the boy's moral development is the acquisition of self-discipline.

Specifics of Self-Discipline

The ability to heed the call of duty, to do what one knows is right regardless of, indeed often in contradiction to, what one feels, is a trait required of all men as they fulfill the office of patriarchy. It is self-discipline that empowers a man to so heed the call of duty. Self-discipline entails the subjugation of one's own inclinations, desires, and feelings unto one's will. Thus self-discipline develops a will that is both master over the mental, emotional, and physical faculties and a servant unto one's duty, ideals, and faith.

In general, self-discipline is a more prominent and intense dynamic in manly formation than it is in womanly development. For though women must discipline themselves, their particular charism is not evoked by the willed hard discipline mandated by cognitive ideals, but rather of a sacrificial love that is evoked by an intuitive receptivity. Where a good man may indeed count the cost of his duty and still do it, and because of this be all the more painfully aware of the price, a woman tends to not count the cost, giving her all in a simpler "fiat." And though a young man too should set his heart, feelings, and romantic yearnings on the most august ideals and causes, so as to facilitate his journey on the high road of life, feelings do not always suffice for him. His feelings are less steadfast but more combustive than a girl's; his heart blazes quickly but often superficially. Therefore it is unlikely that a young man will be able to depend on a constant and correct heartfelt intuition; as such, he often must coerce himself into taking the high road.

Indeed it is the man's lot to supply the objective framework within which womanly intuition is allowed to safely blossom. In building this framework, in defining the context of truth, a man acts in God's stead. He must go beyond that which is natural to the creature, go beyond the natural disposition of pure receptivity (a disposition that is intrinsic to all created persons, but is in so many ways reflected especially in the feminine charism) and conform himself to a standard outside of himself. To so conform himself, he must assent intellectually to standards, requirements, and truths. Often it will be uncomfortable. Often it will entail the burden of duty: the duty of patriarchy.

The end goal of the young man's self-discipline is the formation of the virtues. The word virtue itself comes from the Latin *virtus*, which means "manliness." In acquiring a virtue one becomes habituated in its implementation. Of the four cardinal moral virtues—prudence, justice, fortitude, and temperance—temperance is the most crucial to the young man. Temperance is the ability to govern one's sensual appetites; in short, it is the acquisition of self-control. Purity, or chastity, is an aspect of temperance, and is of chief importance in the moral and spiritual development of the young man.

Procreativity and Purity

Procreativity is the marital trait (the other two marital traits being exclusivity and indissolubility) emphasized in the wielding of the scepter of self-discipline. If during adolescence the newly acquired powers of procreativity are properly ordered, a boy will be well on his way to both manhood and sanctity; for purity forms the cornerstone of manly self-discipline. The outstanding moral theologian Fr. Joseph Rickaby, S.J. (1845-1932), developing a theme of St. Thomas Aquinas', pointed out that impurity's grievous nature stems from the fact that it grossly distorts or mocks holy Matrimony (that is, its specific act) and hence blasphemes that which marriage typifies: the relation and union of Christ and the Church, and Christ and the individual soul.

> Certain actions are wrong, because in them certain types are violated, some sacred symbol outraged, and the dishonor done to the type redounds upon the antitype or thing typified.

> Such I conceive to be the radical reason of the grievousness
> of sin against purity. ... The mischief and malice of such a
> life is not simply in its unhealthiness, nor its undoing of char-
> acter, nor even in its uselessness and injury to the soul, but its
> offending against the symbolism of things mighty and holy.[14]

Impurity is also an antitype of manliness and fatherhood, for
manliness and fatherhood are of the essence of Matrimony. In
fact impurity specifically dishonors and sins against manhood
and the vocation of fatherhood.

If impurity is the specific vice against manhood, then purity
is its specific virtue. Since impurity dishonors manhood, the
key to fostering the virtue of purity is to instill in a young man
an *honor and reverence for his virility*. Indeed, he should look upon
his virility as a sacred trust. This is a momentous task in today's
society, which not only degrades true virility with its basis in
virtue and fatherhood in general, but toys with and mocks procreative powers while at the same time fixating on crass physical manifestations of masculinity. The Western male grows up
in a society that is immodest and pornographic: a society that
is nothing less than idolatrous of secondary sexual characteristics. The task then is to raise the young man to view immodest
or pornographic sights or talk as disrespectful, disdainful, and
destructive of his manhood, as well as contrary to Christian
values. Indeed, such assaults upon manly purity should evoke
passion; not the passion of lust but rather righteous anger.

Such a task is indeed overwhelming from a purely natural
perspective. But the moral virtues, such as purity, are facilitated by the theological virtues of faith, hope, and charity; that
is, they are enabled by grace. Additionally, there is no greater
devotion for the instilling of the virtue of purity than devotion to the Blessed Mother. The young man should be always

---

14. Cited by Attwater, *Op. cit.,* p. 438.

conscious of her presence, and comport himself accordingly. He should render unto her an ardent courtly love, pledging his liege and manhood to the Queen of Heaven. Nonetheless, the instillation of purity requires more than prayer and devotion; it requires mortification of the body and appetites. It is here that the young man must do "violence" unto himself, and embrace the Cross of Christ. He must know Christ crucified through self-control and self-discipline, and view any shirking of these traits as emasculating and disloyal to Christ.

Purity is to be upheld as *the* manly virtue, for upon it hinges a man's dignity, strength, sanctity, and ability to heed the call to Christian patriarchy. The fact that so few men ever master themselves in regard to purity, and hence are ruled by their passions, is the core reason for today's dearth of manly leadership. Indeed, it can well be said that he who is ruled by his lust is ruled by women and their feminine charms.

The process of moral growth and its final end is aptly summed up in this ancient ditty: *Sow an act, reap a habit. Sow a habit, reap a character. Sow a character, reap a destiny.* And it is only he that has acquired a manly character and moral command over himself that is fit to wield the scepter of authority over others.

CHAPTER 5

The Scepter of Authority

ONCE A MAN has done violence unto himself by wielding the scepter of self-discipline over his pride, passions, and flesh, and stands firmly in the presence of God, he is ready to wield the scepter of *authority,* and stand humbly in His stead and govern others.

But even when the proper initiation and moral preparation takes place, and a man intellectually and morally embraces the truths and ideals of Catholic manhood, a sense of inadequacy or unworthiness properly remains. This is because manhood, and its fulfillment in fatherhood, is not something wholly integral to the nature of the creature; for it entails the assumption of an office that is bestowed from without. It is this external nature of the patriarchal office that demarcates such traits as discipline, the heeding of duty, honor, justice, and objectivity as characteristically manly traits.

A father forcefully and sternly commanding his adolescent son to "act like a man" seems proper. Whereas a mother growling out a command for her adolescent daughter to "act like a woman" would seem absurd. Whereas in order to fulfill his manly duty a man must often "act," that is, conform himself to an external standard regardless of his feelings, a woman is most womanly when her acts flow from feelings of love. A woman tends to be more spontaneously intuitive, a man more reflectively deductive. A woman tends to incline towards mercy, a man towards justice. An exhortative, even coercive environment, where discipline and duty are stressed, can work wonders in transforming a boy into a man, but such an environment for a girl would only impede the unfolding of her womanhood. A boy becomes a man by overcoming external challenges and living up to ideals and duties. A girl becomes a woman when the promptings of her biology and heartfelt emotions are gently facilitated or even merely left unopposed. For womanhood and motherhood are natural gifts that will blossom in an environment that is sweet and cloistered; they cannot be imposed, nor does coercion facilitate their development. Motherhood and its genius of receptivity is integral to a woman's nature as a created being; that is, a being dependent on and receptive to the initiation and provision of God. A young girl's womanly gifts are already nestled in her heart and naturally spring forth if they are not opposed.

Manhood and fatherhood, however, will not develop without the issuing of an external call to duty and discipline. The fatherly requirements of initiative and leadership are integral only to the Creator, and hence something external to the nature of man as a created being. This great disparity between the dynamics of becoming a woman, with its maternal virtuosity, and becoming a man, with its paternal virtuosity, can clearly be seen in the culture that in the fullness of time produced the girl who would become the worthy mother of God. In the Blessed Virgin Mary's time and culture a young Jewish girl was able to assume her role as a wife and mother in her teenage years, as was the case with her. A Jewish man however could only assume his full paternal role as rabbi or teacher at an age twice as old, as was the case with Christ.

This disparity exists because a woman is able to heed in a simpler and surer manner her physiology and emotions. A young girl has an instinctual ordering toward motherhood that blossoms as she matures physically; absence an indoctrination or brutalization to the contrary a girl is in tune with her bio-rhythms and desirous of maternity. But a boy's promptings to manhood come from outside himself, and thus becoming a man is a learning process. Because boys and men must seek the ideal of manhood outside themselves there is the male propensity for joining clubs, teams, the military, and even gangs. But although a man's nature is not imprinted with a mandate of manhood, his propensity to seek external measurements or affirmations of his manhood does dispose him to the acceptance of its office and its imposed duties and standards.

In general, it is a good man who will discern what is objectively right or true, using his reason instead of (and often in contradiction to) his own feelings. A good woman, on the other hand, tends to intuitively follow her heart and feelings to discern the right or true path. The man in his objective discernment gauges matters by an external standard. The woman in her subjective discernment is prompted by an internal feeling. Even the often-impetuous wanderings of a man's heart impel him to depend on reason, ethics, and duty, rather than on his feelings, whereas a woman's intuitive heart, when allowed to blossom tenderly, is a sure compass of compassion and maternal love. Both can come to the same conclusion, but, in general, for the man deduction is the surer course; for the woman, intuition.

In God's grand design of salvation, He employs humanity to help bring about His Kingdom. And thus from Adam on, the Lord has commissioned men to share in His fatherhood. But fatherhood is, strictly speaking, *creator*hood. "And call none your father upon earth; for one is your father, who is in heaven."[1] Indeed, there is but one Father, one Creator, one Master, and that is God Almighty. This is why the commission of fatherhood, be it in a familial, clerical, or some other capacity, is one that a man can never be worthy of. Nonetheless, man,

---

1. 64. Matt. 23:9.

frail creature that he is, is indeed commissioned to represent and implement the one fatherhood of God, from whom the dignity and authority of the patriarchal office emanates.

Although familial fatherhood is the natural prototype of all patriarchal offices, it is the holy priesthood that is the ultimate manifestation of patriarchy. For ordination to the priesthood entails a qualitative and everlasting change, whereas other patriarchal offices, including familial fatherhood, entail but temporal commissions. Hence the nature of the divinely bestowed office of patriarchy is made manifest most strikingly in the conferring of Holy Orders. A pious and magnanimous priest, out of reverence for the priesthood of Christ which he bears, will strive to demonstrate a priestly dignity and exercise a priestly authority, and thereby evoke from others the proper respect and deference due to his office. In doing so, the priest realizes that this respect and deference is not merited by him personally, but rather by the person of Jesus Christ. In fact, the more aware the priest is of the unsurpassed dignity of his priestly office, the more aware he is of his own unworthiness to bear such an august office.

It is *not* the priest who is acutely aware of his priestly dignity and own radical unworthiness that asks you to drop the "Father" and call him by his first name. He may do so under the pretense of humility and equality, but in fact he is advancing his person or self ahead of his priesthood. As St. Thomas wrote:

> Even pusillanimity may in some way be the result of pride: when, to wit, a man clings too much to his own opinion, whereby he thinks himself incompetent for those things in which he is competent . . . For nothing hinders him from depreciating himself in some things, and having a high opinion of himself in others."[2]

2. St. Thomas Aquinas, *Summa Theologica,* Pt. I-II. Q. 133, Art. 1.

It is the magnanimous priest, or layman, or religious, who presents his patriarchal office foremost, even at the expense of his own unworthy "self," who is the truly humble man.

St. Joseph was the last and greatest of the Old Testament patriarchs and the first of the new. He is the model for the familial father in his office as the foster father of Christ, and the model of the clerical father in his office as guardian of the Divine. It is St. Joseph's acceptance of his patriarchal office that manifests the proper disposition for all called to patriarchal office. He "accepted with the *obedience of Faith* his human fatherhood over Jesus,"[3] even though, as a mere man, he was infinitely unworthy of that fatherhood. St. Joseph, in virtue of his office of fatherhood, ruled the Holy Family. As head of the Holy Family he accepted not only the wifely submission and obedience of the highest of God's creatures, the Blessed Virgin Mary, but the earthly submission and obedience of God Almighty Himself. With the highest degree of magnanimity St. Joseph assumed such an overwhelming commission because it was his divine duty to do so as head of the Holy Family.

A Wife's Obedience and Submission to Her Husband

No other position of leadership is more absolute than that of the head of the family. The Catechism of Trent declares the full extent of the familial patriarch's claims: "[L]et wives never forget that next to God they are to love their husbands, to esteem them above all others, yielding to them in all things not inconsistent with Christian piety, a willing and ready obedience." The office of familial patriarchy calls for the highest degree of homage, surpassed only by that due to Almighty God;

---

3. John Paul II, *Redemptoris Custos*, Apostolic Exhortation, 15 August 1989, sec. 21.

and it is a man's wife who is properly his first and most loyal subject.

Similar to the teaching on wifely submission is the commandment to "Honor thy father and mother," which again, in precedent of order, is second only to those commandments that pertain to the honor and love of God. Husbands and wives must realize the crucial ramifications of their own marital duty to honor one another, for it is only by following parental example that children are able to follow their grave filial commandment. The husband that degrades his wife by word or deed only degrades himself; for the status of a leader is directly dependent on the status of his followers, and it is a wife who is a husband's essential and first follower. A marriage that is imbued with the spirit of patriarchal hierarchy is one in which the wife is highly honored and never degraded, for the husband's honor is necessarily commensurate with hers. Indeed, as will be seen, the very wellspring of the patriarchal charism is the unique and outstanding *devotion* that a husband has for his wife. Still, it is the mother who is in the best position to edify her children in regard to their filial duty to honor their parents. Not only is she the prime influence on her young children, but she provides a direct example of the spirit of submission. It is the wife's attitude toward her husband, as manifested in even the slightest smile or grumble, that will redound in the behavior of her children. When a wife fully submits to her husband, the children, imbuing this spirit with their very mother's milk, will likewise be submissive.

For modern women, wifely submission requires nothing less than a conversion of heart. In this age of prideful assertion of rights, to submit to another in all things—not only without resentment or exception but with joy—is one of the Faith's hard sayings. As Pius XII beautifully put it,

And do you, O brides, lift up your hearts. Do not be content merely to accept, and—one might almost say—to tolerate this authority of your husband, to whom God has subjected you according to the dispositions of nature and grace; in your sincere submission you must love that authority and love it with the same respectful love you bear towards the authority of Our Lord Himself, from Whom all authority flows.[4]

A Husband's Love and Devotion for His Wife

Yet it is not only modern women that may have a hard time accepting this teaching; modern fathers themselves may find it difficult to graciously accept wifely and filial love and submission. Like the priest who doesn't want to be called "Father," a husband may feel uneasy with or unworthy of such submission and love. He may protest that he doesn't deserve such reverence. He may somehow equate charity with a hyper-egalitarianism that never admits of a hierarchy. Or he may inappropriately use the Lord's exhortation to be "meek and humble of heart" as an excuse for compliance and compromise. He may posture himself in all the above as one following the Christian ideal when instead he is merely weak and devoid of backbone. But behind this pretense of a Christian self-effacement may lurk pusillanimity: an unwillingness, even if unconscious, to respond to that rendered love and submission with the required "greatness of soul" that is the magnanimity of manhood and of patriarchy. For a wife's wholehearted, undivided love and total submission call for a husband's dutiful equivalent response: his assumption of the mantle of patriarchy in total commitment to her and the family. Much as *noblesse oblige* dictates that a monarch

---

4. Pius XII, Allocution to Newly-Weds, para. 82.

is duty bound to serve and protect and rule those that submit themselves to his kingship, so too is a man bound by the
submission of his wife (and her foremost, for she submitted
freely to his headship upon consenting to marry) and his
children.

But a wife's acceptance of her husband's patriarchy requires
more than his mere heeding of the *noblesse oblige* call of duty;
rather it requires that he heed the call of a patriarchal service
and love that is every bit as total as the wife's submission and
love. Pope Pius XII again states:

> But granted this dependence of the wife on her husband
> as it is sanctioned in the very first pages of revelation, the
> Apostle of the Gentiles reminds us that Christ, full of mercy
> for us and for womankind, has sweetened that little bit-
> terness which remained at the basis of the old law. He has
> shown, in His divine union with the Church "espoused in
> His Precious Blood," how the authority of the head and the
> subjection of the spouse can become, without being in the
> least diminished, transformed by the power of love, of a love
> which imitates that wherewith He is united to His Church.[5]

Such a love draws upon all the largesse and nobility of a
husband's patriarchal office, for it is a call to the very greatest of loves: Greater love has no man than this, that a man lay
down his life for his friends.[6] And that is exactly the love St.
Paul requires as the corollary of wifely submission: "Husbands,
love your wives, as Christ also loved the church, and delivered
himself up for it: That he might sanctify it"[7] The duty of patriarchy is summed up in that one verse. A husband is to be *totally
devoted* first and foremost to his wife and then his family: giving

---

5. *Ibid.*, para. 80.

6. John 15:13

7. Eph. 5:25-26.

his all, truly his very life, for their well-being and sanctification. As we shall see in a subsequent chapter, this element of total devotion adds to the Christian patriarch's character of king and shepherd, priest and prophet, that of sacrificial victim.

The corollary and equivalent exhortations for a wife to submit to her husband in all things and for a husband to love his wife as Christ loved the Church express in the fullest manner the nature of true love. True love is necessarily reciprocal. To truly accept another's love one must love him back, for it is this rendering of love that constitutes the very act of accepting the other's love. Pope John Paul II, referencing the union of Adam and Eve before the Fall, said that

[The conjugal] gift consists in reciprocal acceptance of the other . . . in this way mutual donation creates the communion of persons . . . The giving and the accepting of the gift interpenetrate, so that the giving itself becomes accepting, and the acceptance is transformed into giving.[8]

For a man and wife this dynamic of reciprocal love will create a constant flux back and forth which increases both the submission and love of the wife and the patriarchal sense of devotional duty and love in the man.

The doctrine of the hierarchy of the family, then, is not the one-way street it is so often characterized as. It requires reciprocity to enhance its efficacy and bring it to full realization. The hierarchy of the family does not accept the modern prescription of a 50-50 sharing in power between husband and wife, but rather a 100-100 donation of love between husband and wife, with both striving to give their all in accord with their God-ordained roles. This absolute giving of a man and wife to one another is the perfection of the matrimonial state. The Church exhorts both man and wife to love each other with

8. John Paul II, *General Audience,* 6 February 1980.

complete abandon and total commitment, without counting the cost or reckoning rights. And it is the hierarchical order of the family that brings about this fullness of matrimonial love.

Such a mentality of unreserved giving may not be in accord with the twenty-first century Western world's enshrinement of "rights" as the ultimate good, but it is in accord with the Gospel. Nowhere does Our Lord speak of rights; on the contrary He speaks of duty and giving. Christ always said "give," always said to "do unto others": that was His political and social orientation. When one is concerned with his rights he is constantly judging matters by what he gets out of it. He is always on guard lest he get taken advantage of. Such a "rights" mentality is no way to run any organization that requires dedication and teamwork, let alone a family. Such a mentality calls for doing as little as possible, for always counting the cost, instead of doing as much as possible without worrying about the cost. But a Christian is not concerned about the cost of love, for he knows that no matter the cost, even unto laying down his life, Heaven is infinitely worth the price.

The Gift of Marital Procreativity

A man can be said to "give his life" for his family in many ways. He spends his life working so as to provide the essentials of life. He places his life between his family and harm's way to protect their lives. He forfeits a life of self-seeking and freedom for a life of patriarchal duty. But the most basic way in which he "gives his life" to his family, is by *giving life* to his family. Procreativity, as it was with the scepter of self-discipline, is the trait of marriage that is most essential in wielding the scepter of authority.

It is the man's initiative act of procreation that actualizes the maternal vocation of his wife, who is "saved through childbearing."[9] And no greater marvel can a man initiate, nor responsibility incur, nor authority acquire, than the bringing of new souls into existence. As stated by the Catechism of Trent:

> [Fathers] are, so to say, images of the immortal God. In them we behold a picture of our own existence, them God made use of to infuse into us a soul and reason, by them we were led to the sacraments, instructed in our religion, schooled in right conduct and holiness, and trained in civil and human knowledge.[10]

Thus a father's authority is akin to God's, and his responsibilities are ordered toward his children's sanctification:

> Let all be convinced that human life and the duty of transmitting it are not limited by the horizons of this life only: their true evaluation and full significance can be understood only in reference to *man's eternal destiny*.[11]

Of the three traits of marriage, it is procreation that is strictly analogous with fathering. Hence to sin against the procreative power, against purity, is to sin against fatherhood. From masturbation, to contraception, to illicit affairs, to vasectomy, one dishonors his manhood, his fatherhood, and his Christian patriarchy. A man's seed is vital and sacred. Not only is it the product of the hormonal essence of his physical virility, but it is also the sacred trust of his forefathers and his patrimony to his own heirs: the most fundamental means by which he participates in God's creative act. It is often (and rightly) said that contraception degrades women, but it more directly degrades men. It is a man's seed that is squandered; it is his virility that is degraded when his procreative powers are used as a means of

---

9. 1 Tim. 2:15.
10. *Catechism of Trent,* "Fourth Commandment."
11. *Gaudium et Spes,* 51.4.

mere pleasure. No man can sin against his seed without defiling his manhood. Such sins castrate a man spiritually, morally, and procreatively. When a man destroys his seed for the spasms of pleasure and for convenience's sake he is a weakling in the deepest sense of the word.

As sins against the procreative act are specifically antithetical to fatherhood in that they defile the specific act of fathering, so the sin of abortion is specifically antithetical to motherhood. Yet the sin of abortion also entails the father's total failure in his essential duty to protect and provide for his spouse and children. In fact a father's duty to protect and provide is all the more urgent when his wife is with child, as they are both rendered especially vulnerable. When a man allows his child to be murdered in the womb he fails in the most grievous and greatest degree possible as a father.

Manly purity and chastity, that is, the ordering of the procreative powers, is the key to patriarchal authority. If a man is not able to order his virility and thus have it under his control so as to channel it for his spiritual, moral, and procreative strength, if rather his virile passions control him, then after marriage his wife, as the slaker of his lust, will be the one who assumes control over his virility. To such a man the old adage of "his wife leads him around like a bull with a ring through his nose," is most apt, if anatomically inexact.

Where there is lack of manly purity, or a contraceptive mentality—whenever the procreative is separated from the unitive—the establishment of authentic Christian patriarchy is impossible; for sins against procreativity emasculate manhood and eviscerate fatherhood of its dignity and authority. That these emasculating sins against God are accepted and even praised in contemporary Western society, which notably includes the cradle civilizations of Christendom, bespeaks of the utterly depraved state of Western manhood. A new Christendom will never arise unless the emasculation of Christianity itself is stopped and reversed by the establishment of a new order of Christian patriarchy.

The Spirit of the World versus the Spirit of Christ

But to so establish a new order of Christian patriarchy will require militancy and miracles in this post-Christian, anti-patriarchal age. In the popular arena, "patriarchy" is a pejorative, and the mere charges of chauvinism or its ecclesiastical equivalent of clericalism are grounds for conviction. Hyper-egalitarianism is ubiquitous, thanks to propagandizing mass media and enforcement by the modern state, which increasingly intrudes upon the once sacrosanct realm of the family and usurps parental authority. Couple these factors with an endemic extended adolescence and the result is an environment radically hostile to patriarchal authority.

But as contrary as it is to today's sentiments and to the disposition of today's men, the assumption of the patriarchal office is, nonetheless, the grave and sacred duty of Christian manhood. Today to effectively promulgate the values of patriarchal authority it is necessary to clarify that the world's categories of power and control *do not* apply to the Christian ruler. In fact, the world is unable even to *comprehend* the paradox of Christian patriarchy. When the world condemns rulers of the Christian order it says more about itself than about them. For the world understands only one kind of ruler: arrogant, self-interested, and willing to compromise all for the sake of power. But the Christian patriarch does not fit the world's idea of the ruler; rather he conforms to the character of Christ, with His attributes of humility and love and His spirit of self-sacrifice and adherence to truth no matter the cost. St. Augustine put it thus:

But in the family of the just man who lives by faith and is

as yet a pilgrim journeying on to the celestial city, even those who rule serve those whom they command; for they rule not from love of power, but from a sense of duty they owe to others—not because they are proud of authority, but because they love mercy.[12]

The Humility of the Christian Ruler

Humility is the virtue that enables one to recognize and accept the truth about himself. The humility of the Christian patriarch allows him to recognize both the solemn and august nature of his office and his unworthiness, as a mere creature and as a sinful man, to assume that office. So too, humility brings truth always to the forefront and discounts any prejudicial slants of self-interest, and thus allows justice to reign. Although humility gives a Christian patriarch a clear and proportional perspective of reality, it is love that is the driving force behind the implementation of his authority. When authority is wielded by one who loves his charges as Christ loved the Church, even unto giving his life, then all danger of tyranny is removed. The Christian patriarch can thus rule vigorously and decisively, knowing in all humility that it is his duty to do so and that his motives are those of love.

Thus imbued with the spirit of Christ, and heeding not the taunts of the world, the Christian patriarch can magnanimously lead with decisiveness and certitude. And decisive he must be, for, in the case of the familial father, Christian patriarchal authority entails making for the family final decisions of a practical, moral, and spiritual nature. And act with certitude he must, for without certitude he will not develop confidence in himself nor evoke confidence from his family. After having

---

12. Augustine, *op. cit.,* bk. 19, ch. 14.

prayerfully discerned an issue and making a decision, a father hasn't the luxury to be buffeted by doubts that could encumber or disable him as the head of his family. Yet, again, it is not pride or arrogance that causes him to act decisively, but rather it is humility. For the humble man realizes his limitations; he is acutely aware that it is not he who is all-knowing or all-wise. The proud or timid man is incapacitated by his fears of failure; the humble and courageous man accepts the fact that he will at times decide wrongly, that such is the lot of fallen humanity. But the Christian patriarch trusts in God, who commissioned him and gave him his authority. In acting for love of God and family he trusts that the power and providence of God will diminish the effects of his human failings, while blessing those efforts that proceed from his faithful fulfillment of his patriarchal office. And it is humility that will allow him to profit from his failings, and thus grow in sanctity and wisdom.

A humble man is also meek. But a meek man is not a timid or cowed man. Christ was meek and humble of heart and undaunted in His powerful proclamation of truth. A meek man is a strong man, for a meek man is one who has power over anger induced by self-love and pride. He is able to see things as they are—the result of humility—and neither blows them out of proportion because they hit a particular personal chord nor discounts them because they are not personally bothersome. Rather the meek man sees things objectively and reacts accordingly, be that reaction akin to Our Lord's storming of the Temple or His silent suffering at the hands of His executioners. The ability to control and channel one's anger is closely connected with the ability to control and channel one's procreative powers, for anger is often fueled by, and is used as an outlet for, virile energy. Next to impurity, nothing so besots the mantle of patriarchal authority as an uncontrolled, disproportionate, or inconsistent anger.

Too often, indeed most often, a man and father is characterized by a hot temper that flares at small things, such as his child's spilt milk, but responds mildly to larger issues, such as his child's loss of purity. Such a man is known for his riled response to mistakes, minor infractions, and even reports of missed field goals, but is oh-so-mild in response to immorality, mortal sins, and even reports of mayhem and murder. This is because such a man's passion is tied primarily to self-love and pride rather than love of God and family.

No, it is not anger itself that is wrong, but rather inordinate anger in the service of self. Indeed, Our Blessed Lord's cleansing of the Temple is ample evidence of a righteous anger.[13] He acted for love of God, for love of His Father's house, and His ordered wrath was extreme. The Temple area Christ cleared was a massive emporium[14] of commerce and financial transactions that, as such, was also heavily guarded. At time(s) of the cleansing(s)[15] it was also at peak operation. Though merchants and moneychangers are not easily separated from their money, Christ caused the entire emporium to be evacuated with merely a few strands of cord in His sacred hands: a few strands of cord that in effect might just as well have been a .50-caliber machine gun!

When a man exercises his patriarchal authority in humility—with meekness, justice, and courage—he is like the magnanimous monarch who seeks the common good above his own good, but when he gives way to petty fits of anger, as well as offenses against God, he is like the cruel tyrant who selfishly

---

13. Cf. (Matt. 21:12-13; Mark 11:15-17; Luke 19:45-46; John 2:1-12

14. The Temple, which had eight entrance gates, was 1,000 x 1,000 feet, most of which was the Court of the Gentiles where the marketplace was. From 1,000 feet away, a person appears to the human eye as a mere speck.

15. Our Lord Jesus Christ may have cleared the Temple on more than one occasion, since the chronologies of John and the Synoptic Gospels are widely discrepant; near the start of His ministry and near the end, respectively.

abuses his power as well as shirks his duty. Truly it is only the humble and courageous man who can either hold in abeyance the passion of a disordered anger or unleash a righteous anger in a prudent and just manner.

Facilitating Patriarchal Leadership by Seeking Counsel

So too, it is a man's humility that allows him to seek counsel when confronted with a decision that entails some ambiguities. Such a man understands that seeking advice will not diminish his authority, for that authority is based primarily on the office he holds and not on his own expertise or wisdom. And it is properly the wife, as her husband's most loyal subject, who should be her husband's closest and most trusted adviser. For a true follower is not one who is passively dependent on his ruler, but rather one who actively facilitates the leadership of that ruler. A bad follower weighs the leader down, has no initiative, displays neither understanding nor passion for the vision of the leader. Whereas a good follower makes the vision of the leader his own, and therefore is able to take initiative and implement the vision. Indeed, in the case of the family, it is a wife's wonderful gift of nurturing that can cause a husband's vision to bloom. He is the one who outlines the grid of the vision, furrows the field with the steady, strong hand of authority, and plants the objective seeds of ideas; she is the one who waters the field with love, tends the sprouts with maternal care, and gently uproots that which contradicts the vision.

At times a father will also find it valuable to seek counsel from a priest, or some other learned Catholic, who has at hand the teachings of the Church and who can apply them in an integral manner. Yet at no time should the father relegate final decisions to others. The duty of fatherhood requires that he alone take ultimate responsibility for the direction of his family. The temptation for pious Catholic fathers to relegate the decision making process to a trusted spiritual adviser, or for a married couple to argue their case in front of a priest in hope of winning a judgment in their favor, must not be succumbed to. It is the father, not the priest or counselor, who has primacy of authority in the family, and that authority must not be supplanted. Final judgments are always to be left to the father. If he seeks counsel when needed, and prayerfully asks for wisdom, he can be confident that the charism of his fatherhood places him in the best vantage point to make the final decision.

The exception to a husband's prerogative of making the final decision is when he commands something that is "inconsistent with Christian piety." When a priest, within the Sacrament of Confession, hears of a decision or command of a husband that is intrinsically evil, he may so denote it, and even advise the wife to disobey it. But in such a case the husband forfeits his authority by his contradiction of Christ, who is the very source of his authority. There is a great difference, however, between an imprudent or less-than-optimum decision on part of the husband, and an intrinsically evil decision. In the case of an arguably unwise decision a wife is to submit; for it is better to live with the consequences of a less than optimal decision than to live with the consequences of wifely disobedience, a grave sin which undermines the very structural integrity of the marriage bond.

Having recourse to, and a good understanding of, the teachings of the Church, especially as distilled in dogmatic catechisms, is the best means for a father to acquire the knowledge necessary for the moral and spiritual leadership of his family. But knowledge does not suffice by itself; it must be transformed into wisdom by means of prayer and conversion. Only then will a father acquire an integral world view from a Catholic perspective. The studious seeking of theological knowledge and the prayerful seeking of wisdom are not luxuries for the Catholic father. Rather they properly comprise his primary avocation—that is, must be his primary leisurely pursuit—and are essential in his wielding of the second staff of patriarchy, the Crosier.

CHAPTER 6

The Crosier of the Co-Episcopacy

THE FATHER'S AUTHORITY over both his wife and children is derived from Christ. He is commissioned by Christ to assure the material and spiritual well being of his family. In the Christian dispensation it is this spiritual concern that has primacy. A father's highest obligation is to instill his family with the truths of the Faith, and set them on the narrow path to eternal life. His final objective, then, is quite simply the sanctification of his family.

While bishop of Hippo, St. Augustine once addressed himself to a group of fathers of families, greeting them as *"Co-episcopi mei,"* or "My fellow bishops." He then went on to say to them: "Each and every one of you have in the home the bishop's office to see to it that neither his wife nor his son nor his daughter nor even his servant fall away from the truth. For they are bought with a great price." Rightly, then, this aspect of patriarchy is symbolized by the *crosier.*

The Priestly/Episcopal Role

The familial patriarch represents Christ to his family. In this he fulfills a priestly role or, more aptly, an episcopal role; for the familial patriarch's authority is not delegated by a higher ecclesiastical authority but by Christ Himself. Scripture is unequivocal in the familial patriarch's Christological representation: "Let women be subject to their husbands, as to the Lord."[16] So too,

---

16. Eph. 5:22.

the *Catechism of Trent* in delineating the *Duties of Wives* reiterates this direct authority: "Again, and in this the conjugal union chiefly consists, let wives never forget that next to God they are to love their husbands, to esteem them above all others, yielding to them in all things not inconsistent to Christian piety, a willing and ready obedience." (*emphasis mine*).

In this priestly/episcopal role as spiritual head, the father also represents his family to the Lord. This priestly/episcopal aspect of patriarchy can be seen in the preternatural patriarchal office of Adam, who as father, and hence representative, of the entire human family, tragically condemned his descendants to exile by his singular act of disobedience. And it can be seen in the covenants entered into by the ancient patriarchs, and by Abraham, who to this day is a Christian's "father in faith." In the Christian domestic order of patriarchy the father bears the brunt of culpability (for he bears the brunt of authority) before the Lord for his family's actions. It would seem to follow that with this burden of headship would also come a patriarchal charism that makes his fatherly prayers and pleas for his family especially efficacious.

This spiritual headship of the Christian father is not derived from mere physical fathering. Nor is it an authority autonomous to the man, but, again, derives from Christ. Hence in order to be valid a father's spiritual authority must be in accord with Christ's Will. Indeed the entire notion of patriarchal authority is premised on the belief that Christ does indeed give His authority to men. And if Christ gives authority to familial fathers, He surely gives the Church a supreme and unerring teaching authority to guide a father in his patriarchal office. Hence, a father, who requires the submission of his family, must always remain himself submissive to the teachings of the Church. Only in such a union with the Church will his own authority remain intact. It is necessary then that a father be knowledgeable in the Faith, so as to conform himself to the teaching authority of the Church.

Master Catechist of the Family

A father must acquire a solid knowledge of the basic teachings of the Church, not only to ensure that his spiritual leadership conforms to Christ, but also to fulfill his proper role as master catechist of his family. The post-conciliar age has been called "the age of the laity"; the Second Vatican Council asked pastors to "recognize the dignity as well as the responsibility of the laity in the Church," and encouraged the laity "to undertake tasks on their own initiative."[17] And prophetically (even if ironically) so, in the wake of Vatican II a father can no longer imagine that his duty to raise his children in the Faith is satisfied by the mere act of sending them to a Catholic school or to catechism classes. Not only does formal religious education fail when there isn't a harmonious education in the Faith taking place in the home, but there is also no longer the blanket certainty that the formal Catholic education a child is receiving is adequate or even orthodox. As the spiritual head of his family, the father must take final responsibility for his children's catechization.

Where then is the layman to acquire the sure and immutable teachings of the Church, if he is to no longer rely exclusively on others to provide for his children's religious education? It is all written down concisely and clearly in documents of the Magisterium. By having recourse to these documents the father will know definitively what the Church teaches and, hence, be able to teach the Faith with the same conviction and certitude that imbues the magisterial proclamations. And certain he must be in these uncertain times, where messages even from the

---

17. *Lumen Gentium*, 37

pulpit can be deficient or even contrary to Catholic truth. As with all learning, theological study should begin with mastery of the basics which can be found in various catechisms.[18] Along with the dogmatic pronouncements, a father should be familiar with the basics of moral theology, the gradations of theological pronouncements, and understand the difference between discipline and doctrine.[19] For the father is the architect who takes the truths of the Faith, lays out the plan, and oversees the tangible construction of a Catholic lifestyle. It is his chief responsibility to see that the truths of the Faith are enfleshed and that a Catholic culture is brought about in his family.

The Formation of a Catholic Culture

Once a father knows with certitude the facts of the Faith as taught by the Magisterium, he can begin to live them out with integrity, and see to it that they are made manifest in his family's lifestyle. When the truths of the Faith are applied by the laity

---

18. The first catechetical lessons should deal with the teaching authority of the Church. For once one accepts and submits to this authority he needn't explore the philosophical and theological reasoning behind each and every teaching before he can embrace it and commit it to memory.

19. The *Roman Catechism* (the Catechism of Trent) is the definitive dogmatic compilation of the Catholic Faith and most readily yields the basics of dogma. The study of the *Catechism of the Catholic Church* aids in understanding current pastoral approaches, new issues, and as a compendium of scriptural and patristic sources. The *Enchiridion Symbolorum* (Denzinger/Schonmetzer, Herder), which lists conciliar decrees along with condemned propositions (available only in Latin or German/Latin) and *Fundamentals of Catholic Dogma* (Ott, TAN Books), which lists individual magisterial teachings in accord with their degree of certitude, are also valuable references. The papal encyclicals are especially edifying in developing a Catholic outlook on contemporary society. Finally a good manual on moral theology is beneficial, though many that are available today are questionable in regards to the orthodoxy of their principles. A concise moral manual once used widely by the clergy is Jone's *Moral Theology* (TAN Books), which is now back in print.

in their daily lives, then the Faith is "enculturated." Note the difference, as used herein, between "inculturation" (*in* meaning "to locate inside"), which is the adaption of the Faith to already-existing external cultural structures and modes, and "enculturation" (*en* meaning "cause to be"), which expresses the creation or transformation of cultural structures and modes by the integral adherence to and living out of the truths of the Faith. A Catholic culture is one that manifests the truths, values, and beliefs of the Faith, and excludes those contrary to it. By such an enculturation the Faith takes on a tangible nature, and a Catholic culture ensues. This culture, be it confined to a single family or spread through an entire people, is a pervasive Catholic ambiance that is created when the Faith is fully integrated into daily life.

Creation of Catholic Culture is a Lay Competency

But there is no stock blueprint available for the process of enculturation. For the application of the truths of the Faith to one's daily life is a divine art that requires creativity, inspiration, and initiative. The Church provides only the enduring truths and the grace to adhere to them. It is the father's task to lead his family in the specific of enculturation. Indeed, enculturation of the Faith is properly a lay competency. The Church would violate her principles of subsidiarity if she were to micro-manage daily lives. It is the laity that is familiar with the terrain and atmosphere of their homes and their communities. And it is the parents that know the individual make-up of their family members, and their combined communal chemistry. Hence, it is ultimately the father who is responsible for the creation of a familial Catholic culture.

True Christian communities and culture at large, then, arise from the association of Catholic families that take it upon themselves to enculturate the Faith. Pastoral programs that seek to form "parish communities" err if in doing so they usurp the natural role of the laity to form their own communities. For the formation of communities is but the extension of the formation of families. And just as it would be improper for the clergy to be involved in matchmaking or in the parental administration of the home, so too, by extension, it is improper for them to be involved in community-making. It is the duty of the clergy to minister unto lay communities, to provide them with the Sacraments; not to subsume the community under their clerical domain. Again, this violates the principle of subsidiarity and infringes upon the laity's realm of competency. A corollary to this "parish community" error is the over and often improper involvement of laity in liturgical or ministerial duties. Not only do such duties have the tendency to detract from the home, but they tend to restrict the category of a "committed" Christian to those that serve the parish "community" in a quasi-clerical capacity.

It is understandable that such pastoral programs have arisen in a day and age where communities, neighborhoods, and families have lost a cohesive identity. In the past, neighborhoods would produce the institutions that served the community, the center and gem of which was the parish church. Just drive around an old American city and marvel at the beautiful Catholic churches that seemingly rise every few blocks. Proudly erected by their various neighborhoods, parishes then were a manifestation of the community—the community was not a manifestation of its parishes.

It is not the liturgy that is the layman's area of competence, nor is it the formulation of dogma, nor is it even, primarily, catechesis.

And the eleven disciples went into Galilee, unto the moun-
tain where Jesus had appointed them. And seeing him they
adored: but some doubted. And Jesus coming, spoke to
them, saying: All power is given to me in heaven and in
earth. Going therefore, teach ye all nations; baptizing them
in the name of the Father, and of the Son, and of the Holy
Ghost. Teaching them to observe all things whatsoever I
have commanded you: and behold I am with you all days,
even to the consummation of the world.[20]

Thus it is the Apostles and their successors who received
"the great commission." Though the laity may at times assist
in that commission, it remains the specific competency of the
Magisterium and its official and sacramental delegation of the
priesthood. When clergy and laity attend to their respective
duties there is little need nor time for them to cross over into
each other's realms of competency.

The creation of Catholic culture, then, is a lay and fatherly
competency. It is the responsibility and duty of the familial
patriarch to lead not only his family but the Catholic lay community as well. In this duty, however, fathers today too often
take a back seat to their priests and wives. Though the priest
is called to exhort the faithful to conversion of lifestyle and
holiness, it nonetheless remains the familial father's responsibility to detail and enforce particular standards for his family.
Whereas the priest's competency is the Sacraments and doctrine; he should not have to be the substitute head of the family
nor the lay community. Neither are wives to take responsibility for creating Catholic culture. The wife's competency is the
internal care of her family; she too should not have to be the
substitute head of the family or the lay community, for she is
its heart. It is the familial father who is commissioned by God

---

20. Matt. 28:16-20.

to head the family, to set familial standards, and, in conjunction with other fathers, to lead and set the standard for the Catholic community.

There is no excuse for a father's abdication of this co-episcopal duty, for it is he who has the commission and charism to lead the family. It is the father who is charged with applying the Faith to the world and its contingencies. It is the father who must be on the cutting edge of Catholic militancy, especially today when the world rages against the family as never before. Again, when danger threatened the Holy Family itself and leadership and action were required, the angel of God bypassed Our Lord Jesus Christ and the Blessed Mother and spoke to the head of that family: St. Joseph, the Light of Patriarchs.

Conversely, the familial patriarch's specific area of concern is not the ecclesiastical politics that so permeates the Church today, especially in traditional circles. Again, his concern and competency is the creation of Catholic familial culture. Under the leadership of the father, the family's degree of Catholicity is only limited by the willingness of its members. Families can be as Catholic as they choose within their home: in their spirit, thoughts, words, actions, and lifestyle. Above and beyond ecclesiastical politics and the various issues entailed therein, it is in the familial and cultural arena that zealous Catholic families manifest the militancy of their Faith and prove their adherence to truth and tradition.

A Holy Wife and a Cloister Home

St. Paul admonishes husbands to follow Christ's example of love for His bride the Church. It is a husband's duty then to provide his wife and his children with a Catholic cloistered environment. Although such a cloistered environment certainly entails a certain spatial apart-ness from the world it is primarily a spiritual

apart-ness (which the spatial may facilitate) where holiness and
Catholic culture are fostered, and evil and the profane and
secular are excluded. In accord with St. Paul's further exhortation, a husband must be willing to give his very life (as Christ
Himself did) to have such a wife and create such a home:

> Husbands, love your wives, as Christ also loved the church,
> and delivered himself up for it: That he might sanctify it,
> cleansing it by the laver of water in the word of life: That
> he might present it to himself a glorious church, not having
> spot or wrinkle, or any; such thing; but that it should be holy,
> and without blemish..[21]

A holy wife, which necessarily requires a cloistered home,
is the pivotal domestic principle. Upon it the development of
a Catholic lifestyle and culture depends. The most elementary
application of this principle is to resist, if at all possible, the
giving of one's wife over to the world—be it to the corporation or the state—for the sake of a second income. To make
"holy" means to "set apart" for sacred purposes. A Christian
wife is to be set apart for the sacred purposes of the family and
home. Nothing so diminishes the sacred and privileged nature
of the home than when the wife and mother—the very heart
of the home—is engaged in secular pursuits, pursuits that are
unworthy of her womanly attention.

A holy wife necessarily requires a holy place. The home must
be purified of secular and profane values and influences (beginning with those that infiltrate via the mass media), being itself
"set apart" and cloistered. Further enculturation of this foun-
dational domestic principle is to be found in the aggregate of
ordinary activities, which results in a Catholic ambiance, lifestyle, and culture. Such activities should be ordered in accord

---

21. Eph. 5:25-27.

with the valuation of motherhood and homemaking as the fulfillment of womanhood. They should foster in the women of the family an ardent love of home and commitment to excellence in the domestic arts, while diminishing the distractions of external pursuits and activities.

This ideal of the wife and mother must always be upheld as truly the ideal. That is, it must be seen as both normative and exhortative, and it must be a priority. In a manner similar to how fatherhood in its masculine specific virtuosity is the call of all men regardless of actual paternity, motherhood is the call of all women in its feminine specific virtuosity regardless of actual maternity. As Pope John Paul II reiterated, "Motherhood is woman's vocation. It is an eternal vocation, and it is also a contemporary vocation."[22]

As with any divine ideal, because of exigencies there may be at times some exceptions, but these exception must always, even if in an indirect way, in sum finally be ordered to facilitate and actualize the ideal.[23] Thus the family forced by poverty to have the wife work outside the home is doing so as an imperfect means to the desirable end of adequately feeding, housing, and clothing the children. But of course this cannot be done to the detriment of the children's spiritual good, such as having them taken care of by a childcare provider that would harm their faith or morals. Additional and stricter criteria must be applied to those wives and mothers who *freely choose* outside

---

22. John Paul II. *General Audience,* Hall of Paul VI, Wednesday, 10 January 1979.

23. This ideal is diametrically opposed to today's ideology and economical structure, where the two-income family is the norm. Those that deviate from this norm suffer financially. The Church has continually described a "just wage" as that which allows a man to provide for his family by his income alone. Thus a just economy would be one that makes possible the one-income family, and even more so, be one that discriminates in favor of a father or potential father of a family over a single working woman and provides for a fatherless mother and children.

employment or volunteer work. These additional criteria must weigh all the goods of the marriage, family, and children with the highest priority. Because these goods include the more sublime good of a well-ordered, holy, and cloistered home and the good of a home-loving wife who is "set apart" from the profane, such criteria may be characterized as prohibitive.

Core Values Must be Catholic

In order for a father to direct the activities of his family and himself so as to bar the secular and create a Catholic culture, he must have core values that are truly Catholic. One's core values are not necessarily those one *professes*, but those that *in practice* dictate one's behavior, pursuits, and content of life. What exactly is proper Christian behavior, in a given circumstance, is sometimes debatable. What is not debatable, however, is that Catholics must be willing to contradict a world that is increasingly inimical to the Faith. Without a constant growth and striving to be ever more Catholic, a man, or a family, or a community will slowly succumb to the powerful influence of secular society. Catholicism is not meant to be an easy, comfortable religion, nor are its adherents meant to be smug and complacent. If a family's core values are truly Catholic, that family will be, unavoidably, countercultural. The Church gives the highest honor to her martyrs; and Catholics from childhood are regularly encouraged to follow their heroic examples and be willing to die for Christ. But such exhortations are reduced to pious platitudes if the faithful are not willing to accept the everyday countercultural ramifications of following Christ.

It is for the father to prudently chart the course of Catholic enculturation for his family. In the realm of the family he must continually and ever increasingly implement the truths and practices of the Faith in fulfillment of his duty to create a Catholic lifestyle. A father must wield a strong, steady hand at the helm of the family if he is to successfully negotiate the countercurrents of secular society. He must be willing constantly, but gradually, to push the parameters of Catholic enculturation. And he must understand that one can never be "too Catholic," for the more Catholic a man is, the more conformed to Christ he is.

Although the enculturation of the Faith is not an exact science, it does require the formulation and upholding of strong standards. Such standards must be applied with consistency to every facet of life. They must include comportment and speech, attitude and dress, habits of work and leisure. Not one aspect of life should remain unchallenged, for not one aspect of life is immune to the ubiquitous and virulent influence of secular society. An instance of such an "enculturation" of the Faith can be seen in the virtue of modesty. In the current age, pastors of the Church are highly hesitant to prescribe the style of dress required for the proper manifestation of Christian modesty (today one is hard pressed to find such prescriptions even for Mass attendance). Still, the Church's timeless teachings on the virtue of modesty, custody of the eyes, and the occasion of sin remain unchanged. This leaves it up to the Catholic laity to discern and implement standards of modesty by taking the teachings of the Church to heart and living them out with integrity.

For a father to discern the specifics of enculturation requires not only theological knowledge, but a keen and integral Catholic view of life. Such a view of life is also required if a father is to lead his family along the narrow way of the Faith with charismatic certitude and disciplined consistency. His ability to implement in his family the truths of the Faith depends on his ability to make those truths his own. He needs to form a delicate conscience that is sensitive to the presence of sin, and he must strive to heed this conscience if he is to have the integrity required of Catholic patriarchy. It is this integrity that imbues a man with the moral bearing required in effective teaching and leading. A Christian patriarch must see with the eyes of the Christ, ever on watch for the hostile forays of the world: *banishing first the secular and profane from his own heart* and being ever on guard against the unceasing and increasingly vehement attacks against Faith and family.

It is only by conforming himself to Christ that a man can valiantly fulfill the call to patriarchy and successfully repel the internal and external forces that assault him and his family; it is only the grace of conversion that will cause the secular scales of false values to fall from his eyes; it is only by "put[ting] on the new man"[24] that he can rid himself of the remains of a debilitating extended adolescence; and it is only the transforming power of the Cross that can instill him with the deep humility required of the patriarchal office. The call to patriarchy, then, is first a call to *conversion*. The man who aspires to the office of patriarch must gain a Christian perspective of life that is radically different from that of the world. He must be a holy man. He too must be "set apart," so that with a clear vision of the narrow way and a resolute spirit to pursue it, he may lead those entrusted to him through the wilderness of the secular and the profane to their heavenly home.

The Pursuit of Holiness

A man must respond with renewed vigor to the call to holiness if he is to wield the second staff of Christian patriarchy, the Crosier. In so doing, he must be a man of prayer. In addition to the formal prayers that should permeate the day, the Christian patriarch should pray always; that is, his heart should

---

24. Cf. Eph. 4:24

be constantly directed towards Christ, and his mind, even when engaged in secular matters, should be at least subconsciously conformed to the mind of Christ.

The Christian patriarch's pursuit of holiness must be of primary importance in his life. It is even more important than the sanctification of his family. Indeed, it is a man's pursuit of personal holiness that is the best assurance of his family's holiness. A father's words of exhortation or admonition will ring clear and true only when he first has applied them to himself. The standards of conduct and discipline imposed on his family will seem harsh if he himself does not follow standards that are stricter still: personal standards that are nothing less than the standards of perfect manhood, of saintliness itself. The pursuit of sanctity does not admit of half-hearted attempts, but rather is only achieved when every fiber of one's being is committed to the task.

Though a father's intrinsic authority does not depend on his degree of holiness, his efficacy does. A father, like a priest, fulfills an office bestowed on him from above. His authority is from Christ, and is not diminished by his personal unworthiness, so long as he acts in his authoritative capacity in conformity to Christ. But unlike a priest, whose efficacy in confecting the Sacraments is not impaired by his personal unworthiness (for he has the indelible character of Christ's priesthood that not even the most grievous of sins can eradicate), a familial father's efficacy is dependent on his personal conformance to Christ. For a father to efficiently teach, guide, and lead his family he must, by means of his holiness, be an image of Christ.

Marital Exclusivity and the Charism of Patriarchy

The call to patriarchal holiness is nowhere more crucial than in the practice of exclusivity, the second trait of marriage.

Juridically, marital exclusivity is the injunction against having a plurality of wives. Spiritually, which is the full Christian sense, it calls for an exclusivity of heart and affections. It is Christ's call to indissoluble marital exclusivity that distinguishes Christian marriage from all others and raises it to its sacramental status. *Exclusivity* and *indissolubility*, which together with *procreativity* make up the three traits of sacramental marriage, are aspects of the same phenomenon: true Christian marital love. Yet whereas indissolubility does not necessarily imply exclusivity, for in itself it neither proscribes polygamy nor non-exclusive meandering of affection, exclusivity does necessarily entail indissolubility. For when a man gives his heart exclusively to his wife he is preempted from giving it to another in either actuality or sentiment; conversely it is only after a gradual loss of exclusive devotion and affection that a man leaves his wife. Exclusivity, then, in its full spiritual sense, can be looked upon as the interiorization of indissolubility.

This interiorization of exclusivity is essential to the wielding of the Crosier of Christian patriarchy. For it is the man who has integrity of ideals, actions, thoughts, and affections who is able to actualize the full spiritual power and charism of his patriarchal office. It is exclusivity of heart that renders a man pure of heart; and it is purity of heart that is the source of a man's moral certitude and bearing, hence the very catalyst to effective and charismatic patriarchal leadership. A father who is pure of heart has integrity, and integrity is ever so necessary when guiding a wife and children who are by nature and age disposed to intuit, even if subconsciously, the inner man.

Fidelity to the marital trait of exclusivity is the source of holiness for both man and wife. The husband's giving of his life and exclusive romantic devotion to his wife parallels her complete wifely submission to him and exclusive devotion to the home. *Single-hearted devotion to one woman is that which specifically sanctifies the familial patriarch.* The key manly virtue is again that of purity, but now it is emphasized as the deepest purity of heart. A man's exclusive devotion to one woman concentrates, channels, and spiritualizes his virility. It requires discipline and willpower, for it entails a concentration of his affections, and disallows the distractions and dissipations of either debilitating meanderings of the heart or overt and tangible infidelities.

Because it requires not only the external observance of monogamy, but also the internal observance of its principle, exclusivity is the "hard saying" of Christian patriarchy. Fallen man's affections are erratic and easily swayed, and just as easily hidden in the recesses of his heart. But exclusivity requires that a man give all his love and affection—that is, his acts, thoughts, and emotions—to one woman. For the man who lives out fully this principle of exclusivity, as far as the sentiments of his heart go, there is but one woman in the world: his romantic love is intentionally blind to all but his wife. But if wifely submission is a hard saying for women, exclusivity is harder still for men. In fact, it is so hard that it has rarely been implemented and, rarer yet, ingrained in the social fabric of a people, even at the apex of Christian Western culture. It is a sad fact that in the ancient centers of Christendom, and notably in countries predominantly Catholic, the taking of a mistress was and is an accepted way of life.

Since the very source of Christian patriarchy's spiritual power, this radical, evangelical exclusivity was never embraced on a large societal scale, it can be said that never before has there been a culturally established Christian patriarchy. The historical patriarchy in the Christian West, based, as we have seen, on a preexisting pagan patriarchy and rife with pagan values, never reached its full potential in Christ. And in modernity as the final remnants of Christendom were dispelled (this inglorious defeat of Christendom itself an indicator that Christian patriarchy was never truly established), and worldly power structures shifted along lines hostile to it, Western patriarchy, such as it was, withered away.

But a new Christian patriarchy can arise, and this time an authentic one, for it has nothing to base itself upon—neither preexisting societal structures, nor political or secular philosophical ideals—save Christ alone. It can arise if Christian men begin to courageously take to heart the great and radical principles of the Gospel, and specifically the empowering and sanctifying principle of exclusivity. It is indeed exclusivity that will fill men's hearts with the empowering grace and charism of their patriarchal office. It is exclusivity that will specifically sanctify men and render them pure of heart. And it is exclusivity that will embolden men's hearts with the spiritual and moral valor to raise high the standard of Christ amidst the hostile hordes of the world.

But the times are dark, and the world with its diabolical genius militates today as never before against the virtue of exclusivity of heart. Christ said that "whosoever shall look on a woman to lust after her, hath already committed adultery with her in his heart."[25] Today it is the very aim of women's fashion to elicit lustful looks. Truly, our society is nothing less than idolatrous of the feminine body and feminine sexuality. Fashions and behavior that were once considered risqué, or the garb and acts of the harlot, are today acceptable in every stratum of society. And today it is not only the pornographic media that spew forth erotic imagery, but mainstream advertising and entertainment as well.

For the virtuous woman, immodest display of the feminine form is shameful and a weakening of womanhood. But for those women that have lost the sense of feminine modesty, it

---

25. Matt. 5:28.

can be a source of pride and means of power and manipulation. Although a pornographic and immodest society degrades authentically feminine women, it can diabolically empower the unchaste and worldly women, especially when that society worships feminine sexuality. Thus, in a society that caters to male lust, it is *men* that are weakened and shamed. In a pornographic culture it is they that are conditioned from boyhood to respond helplessly to the mere sight of feminine flesh, much as Pavlov's salivating dogs responded to the stimulus of the bell. When man is impure of heart, vacillating in affections, swayed by provocative charms, he is debilitated, and soon enslaved to the feminine.

Pornography and immodesty degrade a man, for they make light of and toy with the powers of his manhood. The Christian patriarch must view immodest or pornographic sights and talk as outrageous affronts to his manhood. He must disdain as shallow and trite the flirtations and frivolous liaisons offered by worldly women. He must not degrade his manhood by allowing his virile affections to be captured by so unworthy an object as the salacious woman.

The sins of impurity range from dissipation to distraction. And though the sins of distraction, or sins against exclusivity of heart, may seem to be of a comparatively minor gravity, they are, nonetheless, seriously disabling for the man who seeks to fulfill the office of Christian patriarchy. For the distracted man is the compromised man and the lukewarm man. Wanderings of the heart or eyes are chinks in his armor; they sap his strength, his very virility, and thoroughly impede his sanctification. And today, the fierce pitch of the battle allows for no such weaknesses.

Custody of the Eyes

It is most crucial and fundamental for a man to develop custody of the eyes, for without it he will never acquire custody of the heart. Even in the most decent of times, men are hard pressed to curtail their contemplation of feminine beauty as they seek to avoid the occasion of sin or the betrayal of exclusivity. But in this day of glossy magazines, salacious videos, and immodest dress, all of which are ordered toward the manipulation of a man's virility, the temptation is greater than ever. Custody of the eyes must be developed to the degree that it entails a near habitual or semi-automatic averting of eyes; that is, one that at least avoids "second glances" when faced with images that affront a man's purity. Although a first glance may at times be attributable more to reflex than to will, a second glance is volitional; and there is a world of difference between a glance and a gawk. As the old maxim told to young seminarians goes, "If you look once you are a man, if you look twice you are not priestly."

It is only by the grace of Christ that exclusivity of heart can be developed, and for men who have grown up immersed in current Western culture a truly miraculous transformation will be required. But transformed hearts must be, for to the degree that exclusivity is inculcated, so too will the strength and spiritual power of Christian patriarchy be actualized. Therefore exclusivity of heart must be inculcated, from the very earliest age. Most fundamentally a Catholic boy should develop a deep devotion to the Blessed Mother as he approaches adolescence; it is the Queen of Heaven that is rightly his first great love. He must realize that his purity of heart and body is the sign of his devotion to and love of the Blessed Virgin. Such a devotion best assures that when he reaches the age of manhood, if the Blessed Virgin should lead him to one of her handmaids, the young man will then be well versed in purity of heart and thus able to render an undivided and exclusive love.

Reciprocally, Catholic girls must be schooled in modesty, both in regards to attire and disposition. They must appear and act remarkably different from women that dress with allurement in mind. All Christian ladies should take to heart the words of St. John Chrysostom concerning feminine modesty:

> You carry your snares everywhere and you spread your nets in all places. You allege that you never invited others to sin. You did not, indeed, by your words, but you have done so by your dress and your deportment and much more effectively than you could have by your voice. When you have made another sin in his heart, how can you be innocent? Tell me, whom does this world condemn? Whom do judges in court punish? Those who drink the poison or those that prepare it and administer the fatal potion? You have prepared the abominable cup, you have given the death-dealing drink, and you are more criminal than those who poison the body; for you murder not the body but the soul. And it is not to enemies that you do this, nor are you urged on by any imaginary necessity, nor provoked by injury, but out of foolish vanity and pride.

For a young man, holiness finds its foundation in purity. For the married man, this purity is manifested specifically in his exclusive love and devotion to his wife. Again, in that very passage where St. Paul mandates the hierarchical structure of the family and husband's authority, he also mandates this exclusive devotion as the corollary of wifely submission: "Husbands should love their wives just as Christ loved the Church and sacrificed himself for her to make her holy." Thus familial Christian patriarchy is intrinsically linked to marital devotion. It is from this very spiritual, ascetical, and even mystical, exclusive marital devotion to his wife that flows a Christian patriarch's charism and vision for leading his family. Indeed, the efficacy of patriarchal leadership is proportionate to the exclusivity of patriarchal devotion. This becomes most apparent when truths gleaned from Church teachings must be prophetically applied and lived out in the unique circumstances of leading a particular family life, and within the larger context of man's exile in this vale of tears.

The Prophetic Nature of Patriarchy

Prophecy is the speaking of the truth and witnessing to the truth as it applies to the times. Knowing the truth and adhering to that truth is the crux of the Christian vocation; it may even be said to be the general human vocation. But it is the Christian who has the fullness of truth insofar as he has Christ, and it is the Christian patriarch's duty to both lead his family in that truth and bear witness to that truth.

Like the collision of hot and cold fronts that results in the fury of the storm is the confrontation of truth and falsehood, the profane and the sacred, the light and the darkness. A Christian patriarch must manifest Christ, the Truth and the Word, not only in the cloister of the home, but in the world. It is he who officially represents his family to the world, it is he who does business with the world. And in the world the temptations to compromise the truth, to acquiesce to falsehood— sometimes due to social pressure, sometimes in the course of making a living, sometimes to avoid out-and-out persecution—are constant. But when a man compromises the truth he compromises Christ and he compromises himself. He trades integrity for convenience, or pleasure, or popularity, or money, or power. The small daily compromises, those that make life agreeable, also slowly eat away at manly integrity. And if a man compromises too much with the world outside the home, he is most likely to compromise the truth within the home. Today it is the rare man indeed who can maintain his integrity; still, by the grace of Christ, the Christian patriarch is called to be that man, a prophetic man of God.

The Christian patriarch must live his life with complete Christian integrity both in the home and outside it. If he does not, then he undermines his ability to lead his family, and children intuitively sense the presence or lack of such integrity. Nothing so undermines the formation of children than the duplicity or hypocrisy of the former. Now, the chief former of a family is the father. Thus the Christian patriarch must guard against the compartmentalization of his life, always holding the ideals of his Faith first and foremost and closest to his heart. In the workplace a Christian patriarch's co-workers should be cognizant of his Christianity and the quality thereof. In practice this means they would be quite aware of his disdain for off-color or impious talk. In more ways than one, the Christian patriarch should not be one of the boys.

Sometimes in the world it is a tough line to walk, discerning when it is best to be silent and when it is best to speak up. But regardless, a man must always be growing in his awareness of that which contradicts or even merely obscures the truth. A man must prayerfully ask for the divine guidance in such decisions, and specifically pray for the gifts of the Holy Spirit, for it is the Holy Spirit that infuses a man's heart and fills it to the overflowing, which is prophecy. With the seven gifts of the Holy Spirit—wisdom, understanding, counsel, fortitude, knowledge, piety, and fear of the Lord—a man will receive both the content and magnanimity required of his prophetic office.

These gifts are needed indeed, not only for the vision they gain but for the courage they entail. For one best witnesses to the truth by adhering to the truth, and adhering to the truth always entails some form of crucifixion: " Jerusalem, Jerusalem, that killest the prophets, and stonest them that are sent to thee."[26] The prophets of old were martyred, as was the Truth Himself, as are Christ's followers who are true to Him: "The servant is not greater than his master. If they have persecuted me, they will also persecute you."[27]

Christ came into the world to testify to the truth,[28] and for that truth He was crucified; and in that sacrificial death the truth was made fully manifest and the Father of Lies defeated. Thus, wielding the second patriarchal staff of the Crosier necessarily leads to embracing the third and final staff: the Cross.

---

26. Luke 13:34.
27. John 15:20.
28. Cf. John 18:37

CHAPTER 7

The Cross of Redemption

NOTHING SO DEMARCATES the Holy Catholic Church from the rest of the world, including other Christian denominations, as her devotion to the Passion of Jesus Christ. It is she who preaches Christ crucified as no others. It is she who upholds mortification, poverty, chastity, and obedience, as virtues of the highest order. It is she who accepts the fundamental and inevitable spiritual truth that there can be no sanctification without suffering. And it is she who takes as her very trademark the symbol of Christ Crucified.

Secularized non-Catholic Christianity tends to lose sight of why Christ came, instead seeing His issuing-in of the Kingdom as bringing prosperity or health or success. But for the Catholic patriarch, whose primary duty in life is to bring himself and his charges to sanctification, it is of utmost importance that he never forget that Christ came not to alleviate suffering, but to elevate it. Christ's Passion did not eradicate the consequences of original sin, but rather enabled them to be the means of sanctification. Man's suffering became the means of union with God in His most magnificent act of love, the Son's sacrificial death. Hence suffering, man's great curse, became man's great blessing.

A Christian father wants to provide for and protect his children. He wants to give them the best: healthy food, adequate clothing, proper education. And rightly so, for it is his God-given duty to provide for them. But he must be on guard against making the procurement of earthly goods an end in itself.

Catholicism does not admit of earthly utopias, but views this world as an exile and vale of tears. The Church refers to herself and her followers on earth as the Church Militant: a Church continually embattled as it seeks to advance the Kingdom. Though she honors the victorious warrior, her highest honors are bestowed upon the victorious martyr. Though she is grateful to the prosperous philanthropist, her royal *professed* religious all take the vow of poverty. Though she joyously proclaims the Catholicity of a large family, the cream of her youth consecrate themselves to holy virginity. Though she champions the human spirit from the arts to politics, her true champions freely choose to submit themselves to religious superiors in strict obedience. Thus, the Church esteems and promotes the goods of the Catholic worldly order while always ordering them toward a higher eschatological good, which often entails their sacrifice.

The Christian father in his love for his children must desire and work for their material well-being. But he prays that it be only in the advancement of their spiritual well-being and that if such material well-being were to impede in even the slightest degree his children's sanctification, it be taken away. A Catholic father must view all his material provisions and ministrations for his children as a process of physical and spiritual maturation that is ordered toward their "hour," their time of sanctity. In stark terms, they are being fattened up and being made ready for the sacrificial slaughter, for the emulation on the Cross that is required of every man who seeks to follow Christ perfectly. Such an emulation, be it achieved heroically here on earth or as the sentence of purgation after death, is what sanctification necessarily entails.

The great Catholic writer Léon Bloy (1846-1917) was once asked what he was bringing his children up to be; he answered immediately: "To be martyrs!" This willingness to sacrifice one's child, be it to the cloister, foreign missions, or into the hands of God, is the most poignant of crosses for the familial patriarch. For mother and father to see their child embracing the Cross is to embrace their own cross most intimately. In this parents begin to understand the disposition of Our Blessed Mother's heart as she gave her *fiat* to Christ's crucifixion. To acquire such a disposition, then, a parent and a Christian patriarch must, like Our Lady, be willing to become one with Christ crucified and to evaluate all worldly things from the perspective of Christ elevated on the Cross and in the light of eternal life.

Suburban Secular Christianity

There is no doubt then as to what authentic Christianity requires in regards to the Cross and the following of Christ: "If any man will come after me, let him deny himself, and take up his cross, and follow me."[29] Yet never has there been a culture so antithetical to the Cross, and thus the Gospel, as that of Western suburbia. The suburban ethos seeks to maintain a lukewarm room temperature that is neither hot nor cold. Extremism of any sort is rejected, unless it is the compartmentalized and superficial fanaticism of sports and entertainment.

The suburban American ethos espouses a culture of superficiality and materialism. Looking good is more important than being good. Being nice is more prized than being right. Being sociable is more important than being truthful. This culture has become globally dominant, fueled by commercialism and the pop culture of entertainment, and spread by the ubiquitous outlets of the mass media.

An authentic Christian perspective does not admit of spiritual complacency. But spiritual complacency is the distinguishing characteristic of the late twentieth-century Western male.

---

29. Matt. 16:24.

For him it is the ethos of suburbia that epitomizes the ideal
of the good life, even if he resides in a non-suburban (urban
or rural) setting. The Western "suburban" male is addicted to
entertainment, which acts as a catharsis for his inner need to
live a life of drama, of battle, and dedication to a cause. How
many men seek fulfillment of their manhood by associating
themselves with a sports team? This becomes the cause and the
drama of their lives: a reprieve of vicarious fantasy that allows
them to endure another week of a visionless, causeless, and
compromised existence. By identifying himself with corporate
athletics and movie fantasies, or as a participant himself in triv-
ial games, the Western suburban male is able to acquiesce to
a society that censures any ardent cause militant espoused for
love of God and the truth. Hence, the Western male in boister-
ous support of his favorite sports team exhibits a bravado: his
voice raises a notch, he speaks with manly conviction. Yet, in
his allegiance to the truth or unpopular principles or Christ, he
is remarkably docile and unmagnanimous: he whispers, and is
ever so willing to compromise. The Western suburban male is
well acclimated to an environment which is spiritually tepid;
an environment where only the lukewarm are comfortable; an
environment that may well be the least conducive in history for
the authentic enculturation of the Faith.

What is there that demarcates the secularized "suburban"
Christian from his non-Christian fellows? The secular suburban Christian, like his fellows, also seeks a place of comfort,
though that place may be adorned with a tasteful crucifix. He
also wants trite answers and so resorts to pious platitudes and
quits questioning. He also wants to be past the throes of growing, of conversion, and so seeks satiation and shuns dying. He
too is bombarded by news and events and political posturing,
and is thus distracted from the real moral challenges of his daily
life. He too is grand-issue-oriented, showing his commitment

to Christ primarily by espousing political and social issues that are outside the realm of his personal sanctification: issues that don't entail crucifixion, at least not for him personally. He may see himself as humble, even as Christlike, in his willingness to compromise on the small issues; the issues that actually touch his life; the issues he actually has full control over; the issues that would actually cost him personally. At best the secularized, suburban Christian is separated from his fellows by a mere code of ethics—a few do's and don'ts—and even that pales in comparison to the codes embraced by many non-Christian zealots, be they religious, politicos, or atheists.

Suburbanism is the American dream, and America dreams for the world through the phantasms generated by Hollywood and Madison Avenue. Suburbanism is also the Calvinistic dream. It is contrary to authentic Christianity to want everything perfect, to fit in well socially, to prosper without a hitch, to live life without the Cross. The gospel of prosperity is a heresy. And it is this gospel that reflects American "spirituality": a spirituality in which the spiritual serves the material. But contrary to Calvinistic ethics of predestination, the chosen man is not the prosperous, complacent suburbanite; rather it is he who resembles Christ crucified, he who is marginalized and hungers insatiably for God and His justice, he who with every spiritual summit scaled faces the dizzying abyss of faith anew.

The journey of faith is about paths, mountains, torrents, and abysses, which increasingly become narrower, higher and steeper, more raging, and more abysmal. The journey of faith leads always and ever further from human and worldly succor. The journey of faith requires steadfast orientating, virtue, and grace, and it is incumbent upon the Christian patriarch to lead the way. He who fails to so lead may do so not so much because he is unsure of his direction, but rather because he is fearful of its ramifications; fearful of giving up the satiation of "the good life" for the life of quest and encampment; fearful of giving up the safety of a measured mediocrity for the onslaught which is the fullness of life in its depths of despair and heights of ecstasy; fearful of giving up the anesthetization of entertainment and lukewarm engagements for the extreme vigor and rigor entailed in being zealously committed to Christ, to the Faith, and to his family.

The Chastised Chosen Man

A man is judged in most societies and cultures by what he does and accomplishes, by how successful he is. This is blazingly true, almost to the exclusion of all other qualities, in Western society, where the "bitch-goddess of success"[30] is worshiped. But a Catholic man should transcend such evaluation, neither being influenced by secular peer and societal pressures, nor, and most importantly, viewing and evaluating his own worth according to such measures. A Catholic man instead ultimately judges himself in the light of Christ. How true to Christ am I? How courageous in promulgating His truth? How manful in embracing His Cross? Such an evaluation must reach to the inner core of his self-knowledge and his masculinity. To so understand oneself entails the process of purgation, the trials of fire. "Take all that shall be brought upon thee: and in thy sorrow endure, and in thy humiliation keep patience. For gold and silver are tried in the fire, but acceptable men in the furnace of humiliation."[31] Acceptance and endurance of the Cross are what demarcate the chosen man, not the material prosperity of suburbia or a secular Christianity's elect.

Self-knowledge means dying to the false or pseudo-self[32],

---

30. A phrase attributed to the American novelist William James (1842-1910).
31. Sirach 2:4-5.
32. See *Imago Dei Psychotherapy: A Catholic Conceptualization* (Dilsaver, 2009)

and not only coming to know the true self, but coming to know Christ, and Him crucified. The patriarch, the chosen man, is called to manifest Christ in word and deed as he leads those in his charge upon the narrow path. But before he can witness to the truth, he must gain the truth, gain the vision, and gain Christ. To so gain Christ he must embrace Him in His agony on the Cross. This is the furnace of humiliation, the furnace of shame. The chosen man is tested by the Lord in the fires of humiliation: so says the ancient scribe to the men of Israel, to the Chosen People. Yet the bulk and leaders of this chosen race rejected the ultimate humiliation of the Cross and Christ crucified, and thus rejected their chosen status. Those that did accept Christ Crucified in fulfillment of God's covenant retained their chosen status, and became the first members of the enduring Chosen People of God that is the Catholic Church. Thus this fulfilled and remnant Chosen People, this Catholic Church, has no covenant and no meaning apart from Christ Crucified.

The Chosen One, Our Lord Jesus Christ, showed the way, the only way of salvation. He—God Almighty, the Second Person of the Holy Trinity, the Son of God—though "Who being in the form of God, thought it not robbery to be equal with God: But emptied himself, taking the form of a servant, being made in the likeness of men, and in habit found as a man."[33] So He showed the way to sanctity, and it is the solemn hard truth that those that follow Him must also be tortured unto death so as to be like our Lord and Saviour. "Can you drink the chalice that I shall drink?"[34] Jesus asks. And He commands: "And calling the multitude together with his disciples, he said to them: If any man will follow me, let him deny himself, and take up his cross, and follow me. For whosoever will

---

33. Phil. 2:6-8.
34. Matt. 20:22.

save his life, shall lose it: and whosoever shall lose his life for my sake and the gospel, shall save it."[35] For a man to seek similitude with Christ, he must be crucified with Christ. This entails the utter abnegation of himself and his utter dependence on God. For such a man, his deepest reality, the core of his being, consists of but two truths. The first is his own utter nothingness, his wretchedness and inability to do anything good, even to exist, on his own accord. This truth is the most powerful reality of his existence, save that of the second. This second truth is the realization that it is not about oneself but about Christ, Who is All-Holy and All-Powerful and Who has an infinite love for one in his very wretchedness. Thus the wretched man contritely turns from love of self to an all-consuming love of Christ. It is the realization of one's wretchedness that brings a man to the crucifixion, to death, to the brink of despair and nihilism, and which makes the realization of the Gospel, the earth-shattering "Good News," possible. These dual realizations come together as the grace-filled penitent embraces the Crucified One as his only hope and only love.

Thus a Christian patriarch is called to stand in the very stead of God, not on his own powers, not on his own achievement, but by virtue of his union with Christ: a union where the furnace of shame and adversity has melded his heart to the Sacred Heart. This is his reality, the essential core of existence itself— Christ and Him crucified—and nothing, not even his love for his wife or children, can cause him to question this unity, for it is the rock-solid foundation of his manhood and essence of his very being. It is this union with Christ that will support him in the days of tragedy that strike every family: when all is dark and his children and wife look to him for fatherly assurance and hope. It is then, when his own heart is broken and bleeding,

---

35. Mark 8:34-35.

that he stands strong and upright; when he stands as father and keeps the hope alive in those that depend on him and promises a new fair day though his own heart is filled with gloom. He can do this for he has been crucified with Christ and hence awaits with certainty the Resurrection. He holds out hope, for nothing can take away his only true possession, which is faith. It is this faith and this hope that a father bequeaths to his loved ones in the darkest hours of life.

Marital Indissolubility

The Cross is there at the beginning as the young man mortifies his flesh and emotions, as he seeks to inculcate himself with the virtues of manhood; it is there as he experiences the deep conversional grace that binds his heart to Christ's; later it is there as he stands in the stead of God the Father and makes the hard decisions for his family and bears the lonely burden of responsibility; it is there as he stands strong and hopefully for his family in the face of tragedy; it is there as he prophetically witnesses to the truth; and it is there too as he grows ever-deeper in love with his wife. For Christian marriage is a sacrament ordered toward sanctification, and without the Cross there can be no growth in holiness. The couple may spend the early days of their marriage in the fragrant, fecund garden of new love; but for this love to grow they must soon walk the arid paths of the garden called Gethsemane, there to find and follow the Lord and discover a new trysting place at the foot of the Cross. It is there that their love, transplanted now in the precious, crimson soil of Calvary, comes to full fruition in Christ; it is there that they reach sanctity as one.

Indissolubility is the third of the three traits of marriage: the lifelong commitment of matrimonial union given to God and one's spouse. It is a commitment to an ideal, a relationship

modeled on that of Christ and His Church, and one of practi-
cality encompassing the everyday events of the human condition. And it is this trait that most coincides with the third staff
of patriarchy, that of the Cross; for the vow of indissolubility
requires a married couple's steadfast commitment to grow in
love regardless of obstacles or vacillation of the affections.

True love is indissoluble love. Hence true love must find its
ground in that which itself is indestructible. To love a person
for her accidentals, be it her hair, her smile, her "this" or her
"that," is not to love the *person* at all, but rather accidental, transitory aspects of her. True love for a person goes beyond the
transitory and loves the soul that informs the body. It is this
love that is indestructible. But true love, be it for God, or for
one's spouse—and the Sacrament of holy Matrimony includes
both—comes into being only through times of trial. True love
means that no matter what, "in sickness or in health, in poverty
or in riches," I will be one with you. It means that even though
it entails my very crucifixion I will be one with you. And if the
sacrament of holy Matrimony is to fulfill its end of sanctification, it must entail crucifixion.

Familial Poverty, Chastity, and Obedience

The establishment of a Christian patriarchal home entails
a marked discipline and ethos of life. Such a discipline and
ethos will entail accepting the fundamental suffering of human
existence, as well as the specific suffering entailed in family
life. Such a discipline and ethos will also entail the choosing
of pious and mortifying practices. These pious and mortifying
practices are done in the pursuit of sanctity, and seek to exclude
the profane and occasions of sin as well as prudently giving up
of things that are good in themselves for love of Christ.

Ordinary Catholic familial life is necessarily ascetical. With the ongoing acceptance of the deep sorrows entailed in mortal existence, the joyful acceptance of the ordinary crosses of familial existence make up the essence and bulk of all familial asceticisms. Such ordinary crosses entail the moderate sicknesses, the conflicting temperaments, the venial sins, the maintenance of hearth and home, the feeding, the chores, and the myriad of inconveniences that an ordinary familial existence entails. When such crosses are embraced with a full and ungrudging "yes," they are indeed sanctifying.

The foundation of these ordinary crosses is found in the consequences of original sin:

> To the woman also he said: I will multiply thy sorrows, and thy conceptions: in sorrow shalt thou bring forth children, and thou shalt be under thy husband's power, and he shall have dominion over thee. And to Adam he said: Because thou hast hearkened to the voice of thy wife, and hast eaten of the tree, whereof I commanded thee that thou shouldst not eat, cursed is the earth in thy work; with labour and toil shalt thou eat thereof all the days of thy life. Thorns and thistles shall it bring forth to thee; and thou shalt eat the herbs of the earth. In the sweat of thy face shalt thou eat bread till thou return to the earth, out of which thou wast taken: for dust thou art, and into dust thou shalt return."[36]

The asceticism involved in the choosing of pious practices and mortifications can also find its roots in original sin, for it seeks to remedy the darkened intellect, weakened will, and heightened concupiscence that are part of man's fallen nature. And all the suffering of the faithful Catholic becomes no longer a curse but a blessing in Christ for it is the means of the Cross of redemption and sanctification.

---

36. Gen. 3:16-19.

The locus and implementation of familial asceticism resides first with the father, and then with his wife. The children and other members of the family partake in the spirit of these values by being gently directed to the service of Faith and family and relinquishing lesser goods in their choosing of the highest goods as prescribed by the Holy Catholic Church.

As in other areas it is the father who must lead in the realm of self-denial, asceticism, and penance. Indeed, the Christian patriarch must embrace a penitential lifestyle, for his family, himself, and the Church. For in these times are times of cataclysmic challenges, Christian patriarchs must be the fathers of saints, defenders of the besieged family, veritable knights in the service of the Faith. Rightly, then, familial asceticism asks more of the father than any other member, and asks that the father go beyond the Church's minimal prescribed asceticism to embrace ever-greater disciplines. When at the dinner table the milk is inevitable spilled, does the Christian patriarch say "yes" to this small but often surprising sharp pain to his will? If not, how will he say "yes" to the spilling of the very blood of martyrdom?

Familial asceticism shares in the charism of the evangelical counsels, but is not as radical, due to the exigencies of familial and secular life. Nonetheless, familial asceticism entails a certain poverty, chastity, and obedience, which when practiced best dispose children to discern and follow the call to enter consecrated or priestly life.

Poverty

Familial poverty seeks to create and maintain a home that is cloistered and holy. It specifically rejects consumerism and it works toward a simple self-sufficiency that minimizes expenses and cash flow. In addition to the premium it places upon home-making and a mother's being singularly dedicated to her family, it also recognizes the desirability of subsistence food production, cottage industries and even, if possible, a father's working from or in close proximity to home.

Family poverty also entails limiting the influence of popular culture and entertainment. Thus, at the very minimum, the television, computer (both games and internet), videos, movies, music, and reading material are to be strictly monitored. When popular entertainment or literature is being considered it must be evaluated as to whether it is contrary, neutral, or edifying in regards to bringing one closer to Christ. That which is contrary must be forbidden, that which is neutral should be curtailed, and that which is edifying allowed. But even edifying entertainment can carry with it the harmful effects inherent in being passively entertained, thus conditioning a child to the ready acceptance of the influence of, and the desire for, the mass media.

With familial poverty, the father's duty is to lead the way by limiting or giving up pursuits of entertainment, sports, and games: activities that define the secular male ethos in these times. If engaged in, athletic pursuits should be ordered toward keeping fit and maintaining a man's physical and moral disposition as provider and protector of his family. Casual play with one's family is encouraged, as are hobbies that are part of life skills, such as hunting and fishing, so long as they are not disproportional.

Chastity

The second familial asceticism is that of chastity, which involves a heroic openness to life and a commitment to purity and exclusivity, as we have seen. It also entails the following and facilitating the individual charisms of the male and female sexes. Christian patriarchal families should be careful to avoid that which harms the charisms of their sex, such as girls playing territorial or aggressive sports, or boys being too coddled or overprotected.

Familial chastity also entails proper dress. Although many Catholics realize the importance and propriety for clergy and religious to dress in accord with traditional standards, they should realize as well the importance for their own dress to befit their dignity as Christian men and women. In regards to women's dress, much has been said by the Church[37] in the past and has been reiterated in traditional circles, and the familial patriarch should seek such guidance in setting and fostering the standards of dress for his family.

But the familial patriarch must also lead the way in this asceticism of dress by himself dressing in accord with the traditional standards of the Christian gentleman. As such, men should hold as an ideal the modesty of full trousers and shirts as a corollary to the ideal of a woman's full skirts and blouses. The wearing of suits or sports jackets is also an ideal, for in Western civilization full dress for a man has always included an outer-garment, be it the cloak over the toga that Our Lord wore or the modern suit jacket. This fullness of dress is especially proper (and at times mandated by the Church) at liturgical functions.

Finally, the wearing of irreproachably Catholic and sex-appropriate attire should be seen as a marvelous opportunity to witness to the world. By the mere means of one's dress one can be both a Christlike inspiration to others and a militant witness against the profane popular culture. A woman, especially, who always dresses in accord with the timeless Catholic

---

37. Under mandate of Pope Pius XI, the Vatican's Sacred Congregation of the Council (Jan. 12, 1930) issued guidelines to all bishops on the subject of women's dress which was reiterated by the Cardinal Vicar of Pius XII (Imprimatur dated Sept. 24, 1956): *"A dress cannot be called decent which is cut deeper than two fingers breadth under the pit of the throat; which does not cover the arms at least to the elbows; and scarcely reaches a bit beyond the knees. Furthermore, dresses of transparent materials are improper."*

standards integrally witnesses against the egalitarianism and feminism of the world while manifesting the true charism of Marian femininity. A man, too, when he dresses in a mature manner, witnesses against the extended adolescence that infects contemporary men while manifesting the solemn office of Christian fatherhood.

Obedience

The final familial asceticism is that of obedience. As been elaborated upon elsewhere herein, familial obedience entails wives being submissive and obedient to husbands, and children being obedient to their father and mother. For the Christian patriarch, obedience requires submission to Christ and the Church. A Christian patriarch can only speak or act with complete certitude when what he says or does is harmonious with Christ and Church teachings. The Christian patriarch's obedience means a circumspect submitting to secular, legitimate authority as well.

But a Christian patriarch can never submit to another human authority (even be that authority a priest or Bishop) in abdication of his own responsibility and authority for his family. Rather, the Christian familial patriarch must inform his conscience the best he can with Catholic principles (a process that would best include the counsel of the clergy). Unlike a religious under obedience—or a wife—the Christian patriarch has not the luxury nor option to defer his decision making to another. Indeed, the Christian patriarch submits first and foremost to Christ and His Truth.

Unlike much of non-Catholic Christianity, which depends on the personal qualities (e.g., preaching, scholarship, or charisma) of its religious leaders, Catholics are not respecters of persons but rather of office. Even a Catholic's faithful submission to the Roman Pontiff is not a submission to the man who is Pope but to the office of the Vicar of Christ held by the particular man, an office that requires submission regardless of the worthiness of the office holder. *Absolute* obedience is to be rendered only unto God.

Thus the Christian patriarch must lead the way in emulating Christ, willing to be obedient even unto accepting death. It is with Christ that he must learn to say "not my will, but thine be done."[38] both in the daily inconveniences and ordinary travails of life as well as at the hour of his darkest trial.

The Royal Road of the Cross

To hope when his heart is broken, to believe when all is dark, to love when that love means crucifixion, this is the call of the Christian patriarch. But long-suffering takes a heavy toll, especially on men. Fathers are charged with rectifying, alleviating, and remedying. But fathers are only human, and when they are unable to rectify, alleviate, or remedy they are pained by their failure, even if this failure is beyond their control. Men are made to fight and control a situation, and when they cannot or the effort is futile, they are often broken in spirit. But for the Christian patriarch, being broken in spirit should be seen as being broken in all self-reliance and pride. Though he be utterly devastated in his natural manhood, if the Christian says "yes" to this devastating pain, the enduring spirit of Christ will wax within him. "He must increase, but I must decrease."[39] Yes, the man will be broken, becoming less even unto nothingness, and in his stead Christ will rise, becoming ever more. The Christian patriarch must with each setback, failure, or catastrophe abandon himself fuller to Christ and offer up his suffering in union with His. The spirit of Christ can never be broken no matter

---

38. Luke. 22:42
39. John 3:30

the failures, no matter the defeats. Indeed it is the failures and defeats that provide the greatest means of sanctification and thus allow a man in the throes of this sanctifying purgation to continue to "fight the good fight" on the very deepest and most efficacious level.

What is victory, what is defeat, when judged in light of the Holy Cross? The world's standards are not God's. What of the catastrophic defeats that have visited the Church over the centuries? The schism, the confiscations, the apostasies, the failures. And yet isn't the Kingdom just as surely coming? And what of the Lord's own apparent defeat on Calvary, a death as ignominious as imaginable, and of His scattered disciples? A Christian patriarch must know that the only lasting defeat is that of despair, which is, quite simply, surrendering to the forces of Hell. A Christian patriarch can never surrender to Hell, but he must surrender his pride and self-love up to crucifixion. If he does so he will go the distance no matter the buffeting, no matter the knockdowns. If he repeatedly gets back up—that is, if he is continually reborn after dying to himself—and endures till the final bell tolls, he will be victorious in Christ.

It is devotion to the Holy Sacrifice of the Mass that best imbues a man with the capacity to suffer. For the sacrifice of the altar, where Christ's death on the Cross is made present, is the only source from which the forgiveness of sins issues forth. A man's own sins, the sins of the world, original sin itself with all its consequences of natural suffering, all are subsumed by the Lord and bled out in the expiation and purgation of the Cross. The Mass is the essential wellspring of the grace of Calvary. It is only on the altar of sacrifice that the malignancy of sin is dispelled, only there that the brutality of suffering is made endurable, indeed transformed into the very means of sanctification. And insofar as a man partakes in the Lord's Passion and death, he becomes sanctified and like unto Christ, and Him crucified.

To the degree that he enters into the suffering of Good Friday so too will he enter into the joy of Easter Sunday. And kneeling at the foot of the altar, as he eats the Lord's once-scourged and crucified flesh, and drinks of His once-spilt blood, the communicant does not shun the Cross, but proclaims his desire to become one with the crucified Christ.

No man can fulfill his duty as patriarch, or indeed as a Christian, without walking the royal road of the Cross. And when a man's knees quake and his heart pales on this royal way let him have recourse to the Blessed Virgin Mary. For he too needs to depend on someone, he too still needs the comfort of a mother. Let the brave Christian patriarch be not ashamed to embrace her as he walks his own way of the Cross. Let him lean on her, so that others may lean on him:

> *Hail, holy Queen, Mother of Mercy! Our life, our sweetness, and our hope!*
> *To thee do we cry, poor banished children of Eve, to thee do we send up our sighs, mourning and weeping in this vale of tears.*
> *Turn, then, most gracious advocate, thine eyes of mercy toward us; and after this our exile show unto us the blessed fruit of thy womb Jesus;*
> *O clement, O loving, O sweet virgin Mary.*
>
> *Pray for us, O holy Mother of God:*
> *That we may be made worthy of the promises of Christ.*

CHAPTER 8

The Heart of the Home

PRIDE AND SELF-LOVE[40] are the great blights of Christian patriarchy, turning a Christian patriarch into a tyrant and causing a wife to rebel. But pride and self-love find their antidotes in humility and charity, which must permeate the Christian patriarchal home and the hearts of its members.

Poetically and piously speaking, it is in the heart that pride and self-love as well as humility and charity reside. Much has been said in previous pages about the sort of heart a Christian patriarch must have. But he must also facilitate and cultivate the sort of heart his *wife* must have, she who provides the mortal heart of the home. Just as it is the patriarch's office to represent Christ as the priest, the prophet, and the king of his family, so too it is the wife's call to manifest to the family Christ's Sacred Heart in her own heart.

The essential way for a man to cultivate in his wife a humble, charitable, and indeed sweet response to patriarchal headship is for him to wield his authority in a humble and charitable, and indeed gentle manner. Of utmost importance in this is for a husband to be on guard against an *over-reactive implementation* of his patriarchal authority. When rectifying a deficiency or vice there is often overcompensation. Those seeking to fulfill their office as Christian patriarch (again, especially in light of today's generation being the least suited for such a fulfillment) may

---

40. See *Imago Dei Psychotherapy* (Dilsaver, 2010). Self-love here refers to any inordinate love of self, that is any love that does not ultimately find its end in God rather than self. This love of God is charity.

be uncertain and fearful of the efficacy and consequences of their leadership and thus tend toward tyranny or bullying in overcompensation.

An example of overcompensation can be seen in the virtue of courage, which a virtue most crucial to Christian patriarchy, and its deficient vice of cowardice and excessive vice of recklessness. Here a cowardly man, in an effort to become courageous, may act recklessly. Thus a cowardly soldier dominated by his fear may seek to escape it by recklessly charging the machine-gun nest and be promptly mowed down. Contrast this to the soldier who though fearful is not dominated by that fear, but rather, moved by reason and duty will calculatingly make his way into position so that he may best put the machine-gun nest out of commission, even if, in his calculations, he may have little chance of survival.

Like many excess vices, the recklessness of a blindly-charging soldier appears more like the courage of a hero's actions than does the cowardice of a soldier quivering in his foxhole. However recklessness is still an irrational reaction to the emotion of fear, and therefore lacks prudence—and usually efficacy as well. A similar dynamic can be found in the character of a king or patriarch: whereas the tyrant in his excessive dominance is more king-like than a mere figurehead in his powerless deficiency, the tyrant nonetheless still lacks in virtues such as justice and mercy. This lack of virtue not only makes the tyrant vicious but invalidates his authority, in that vice countermands God.

The Christian patriarch's leadership, likewise, will not withstand the countermanding of God. Thus he has no authority to command something contrary to faith or morals, and must be opposed if he does so. But the issuing of an invalid command to sin would seem to be very rare instance by a man who recognizes that his authority comes from Christ. More likely to occur will be the vicious implementation of patriarchal

authority for a licit request. Although the vicious implementation of authority does not invalidate that authority, nonetheless,
it greatly diminishes its efficacy. The vicious implementation
of patriarchal authority, even for just commands, is animated
more by pride and self-love than love of God and family, and
is especially liable to occur when a Christian patriarch's just
orders or expectations have not been met; then an anger fueled
by wounded pride causes the Christian patriarch to act impru-
dently, or ineffectively, or even sinfully.

To safeguard against such an excessive overcompensation
(again, one that today's men may be especially prone to due to
their baseline deficiency in manly and patriarchal virtue), the
fledgling Christian patriarch must be able to fully accept, indeed
welcome, the inevitable wounding of his pride and self-love. It
is a prerequisite for sanctification: I must decrease and He must
increase. It makes possible patriarchal, sacrificial love: love your
wives as Christ loved the Church. And it makes possible the
complete self-immolation of the Christian patriarch for his
family: no greater love than to lay down his life for his friends.

And it is the humble and charitable heart that best facilitates
effective leadership and represents Christ the King: be ye meek
and humble of heart like me. Such leadership is of a moral quality whose force is that of truth and love and as opposed to fear
and coercion. Evoking fear itself utilizes a follower's self-love
and pride: the preservation of self.

The Christian patriarch must not give in to the fear that
comes from threats to his own pride and self-love, a large
part of which may stem from his wife's or his children's very
resistance to his leadership. Risking to lead invariably leaves a
man's pride vulnerable. This vulnerability must be *fully accepted,
indeed welcomed*. For any diminishment of pride, even when it
comes from resistance to leadership will, paradoxically, facilitate that leadership. Once a Christian patriarch no longer fears

the diminishment of his own pride and self-love, but rather welcomes the humiliation, he can then be sure to utilize even anger prudently and justly, for it will be an anger evoked for love of God and others.

The Predominance of Familial Matriarchy

Thus the best way for a Christian patriarch to facilitate a wife's diminishment of pride is to accept his own humiliation. And he can be assured that as he assumes his leadership role there will be plenty of opportunities to experience the humiliation of resistance and even rebellion. Even many conservative Catholics who abide by the minimal required moral code set out by the Church, that is the list of "do's and don'ts," and consider themselves ardent Catholics because they do send their children to Catholic schools or don't contracept; even they (men and women) often bristle at the mere mention of a patriarchal order. They may even be consider themselves traditional Catholics, and fret about the liturgy or the general state of the Church, but would never consider putting their own domestic order in line with the ancient teaching of familial patriarchy.

Christian patriarchy today has been decimated, above all because lay Catholic men have shirked their patriarchal duties. Because of this, many Catholic women may simply be doing their duty when they fill the void left by abdicating husbands. Pius XI speaks thus:

> If the husband neglects his duty, it falls to the wife to take his place in directing the family. But the structure of the family [patriarchal hierarchy] and its fundamental law, established and confirmed by God, must always and everywhere be maintained intact.[41]

---

41. *Casti Connubii*, para. 28

Pius XI here demands of women a difficult and delicate maneuver (though one the feminine genius is well suited to): that even as they fill that void of patriarchal authority, they must never cease to seek ways to facilitate the re-installation of their husbands as manifest head of the family.

Yet in addition to those women who with reluctance take on the leadership of the family, there are also some who relish the leadership and would be loath to relinquish it. Whatever the mixed proportions of abdication and usurpation, the sum result is that *popular Catholicism is now a matriarchy,* especially in regards to the all-important spiritual and moral headship of the family. It is mother who more often than not is the one who has the spiritual vision and the delicate moral conscience, and provides the piety. Father may still be decisive in regard to finances, but not in regard to romances. He may still lead in regard to family vacations, but does not facilitate religious vocations. Father may still be a zealous exhorter of his children to excel in athleticism, but is a sheepish dullard in exhorting towards asceticism. He may vigorously work on the maintenance and improvement of the family home, but is most lazy in maintaining and improving the family members' interior castles.

This book has throughout addressed these men who shirk their most important patriarchal duties. But what of the aspiring patriarch who faces a wife reluctant or resistant to his headship? As long as a wife has some vestige of pride and self-love, there is going to be hurt and at least a temptation toward resistance. This is where the leadership of love and acceptance of humiliation comes in, as represented in the carrying of the patriarchal Cross.

Some zealous Catholic women may even on principle be unwilling to surrender their authority. Here the Christian patriarch must take up the Crosier to instruct and exhort. And note well, he needn't be smarter or even wiser than his wife, for in addition to his patriarchal charism, his lesson is true and this truth will make up for his deficiencies as long as he stays with that truth. He must first convey to his wife how lack of patriarchy leaves Catholics unable to unite into strong communities. (In that it is the God given nature of a woman to care first and foremost for her own family, matriarchies are too concerned with their own to be justly concerned for the whole.) A matriarchal Catholicism is an eviscerated Catholicism, unable to militantly advance the Kingdom of Christ in a world militantly opposed to it. Therefore, it should be the Christian woman's most ardent prayer that the patriarchal hierarchy of the family, both in her own home and in the wider Church, be quickly and firmly established. The Christian patriarch's wife must be convinced that she is called to order her prayers, sacrifice, submission, and love to the strengthening of that order and her husband as he heeds the urgent call to a new Christian patriarchy. And the Christian patriarch must himself remain convinced of and hold fast to these truths, regardless of resistance.

But it is not only in ideological gestures that the patriarch assumes his headship. He reinforces that headship in the small things. For instance, though many families are in the habit of letting their children lead different decades of the Rosary, wouldn't it be more edifying for the husband to lead through-out, as is the common practice when a priest recites the Rosary with the laity? Or, wouldn't it reinforce immensely the spiritual headship of the father if he were to lead morning and night prayers, and end each with a patriarchal blessing of the home and each individual member of the family, starting with the wife?[42] It is the small routine acts such as this that help establish

---

42. Prayers can be found in the Divine Office for morning and night blessings, and

a father's spiritual headship. On the larger level, as we noted in chapter six, a man should be the spiritual director of both his wife and children. Though fathers will differ in aptitude and knowledge and hence competency in fulfilling this role, they nonetheless should strive to do so to the greatest extent feasible, and again can be assured of the requisite charism to do so.

Patriarchal Devotion to the Wife

A Christian patriarch serves with all his might and main the cause of Faith and family. Within the recesses of both Faith and family is found the heart of the matter. The Faith's heart is the Most Blessed Sacrament. The family's heart is the wife and mother. A man's religious devotion is to be centered on the Eucharist and his familial devotion is to be centered on his wife. The love, honor, and devotion shown to these hearts reflects a man's overall commitment and allegiance to the twin cause of Christian patriarchy.

A man's devotion to his wife, as St. Paul says, is to make her "holy and spotless." A man seeks his wife's pristine sanctity, knowing full well that his sanctity is intrinsically tied up with hers. As such he loves her as he "loves his own body," and more since he is willing to sacrifice his very life for her. Though the head of a traditional Catholic family may have to deal with the profane, and devote time and energy to the secular, he has the consolation of knowing that his wife, flesh of his flesh, is peacefully cloistered within the undefiled Christian home and singularly engaged in the lofty vocation of family life.

It is within the home that the most splendid fruits of human

---

adapted for family use. Individual blessings may, for instance, take the form of tracing the cross with holy water on the forehead of family members with the words: "May the Lord bless you, protect you from all evil, and bring you to everlasting life."

existence blossom; indeed it is this domestic fruition to which a man's labors are finally ordered. In the home, where the drama of life is lived out in all its richness, one can be truly human, truly oneself, spontaneous and without need of pretense. There one can unabashedly celebrate and revel in life's profound and simple joys or mournfully enter into the mystery of its deepest sorrows. There one can be as Catholic as one desires, with no need for compromise. And there in the home, the sublime process of sanctification slowly but surely takes place. In sum, it is the home where life can be *lived to its fullest*. Hence the Christian home is to be a place free from worldly aggression, power plays, and contention. It is to be a place of unity, love, and harmonious hierarchy. Accordingly the Christian patriarch must cherish first and foremost the woman of that home, who is its very heart. He must set her apart from the profane so she may flourish in modesty, gentleness, and holiness. And the Christian patriarch must strive to make it possible for his wife to be exclusively devoted to her home and family.

A woman's place is in the home not because she isn't good enough for the world, but because she is *too good* for it. When she gives herself to the making of a dollar rather than a home, a woman's precious gifts are squandered. The world's corporations, bureaucracies, and agencies are profane entities that are unworthy of a woman's devotion and unable to value the feminine charism. These profane entities coarsen, poison, and suck dry the maternal heart. "Martha, Martha, thou art careful, and art troubled about many things: But one thing is necessary. Mary hath chosen the best part, which shall not be taken away from her."[43] Mary had chosen contemplation, the only way of life that is even less worldly, even more feminine, than that of mothering and homemaking. What would Our Lord say to the

---

43. Luke 10: 41-42.

woman who has even abandoned the family, her children, and the home, and is troubled about many worldly things?

Note well that Christ is not condemning Martha's tangible endeavors, but validating Mary's intangible ones. Indeed, it is in the context of Martha's well-ordered home that Mary is able to encounter Christ most intimately. Also note that Mary does not forsake her maternal vocation even though she does not experience physical maternity, for as His Holiness John Paul II often reiterated, *motherhood remains woman's eternal vocation.*

The accomplished, refined, and holy woman dedicated exclusively to the home is a great witness to the world even in her anonymity. Where she could utilize her talents for the sake of gaining the world or even for the sake of serving the world, instead she stays hidden within the cloister of domesticity; her talents used exclusively for the creation of a single sphere of holiness, a sphere that is indeed the basic cell of both Church and society. She shapes souls and hence destinies in her quiet, paradoxical undertaking. She contradicts the world today just as the religious monk or nun contradicted it yesterday. She manifests in her choice of life the kingdom of God.

No, the Catholic wife and mother does not exist for this world, for its rewards, its trinkets of success. She exists exclusively for the Kingdom of God and for the bringing forth of holiness. Indeed, her choice, relative to the choice of careerism, is indeed a choice to live in poverty, chastity, and obedience. She chooses in the spirit of evangelical poverty to give up the glamour and gains of the world, to forgo two incomes for the priceless treasure of domesticity. She chooses in chastity to give herself to the role of motherhood, to open herself up to life, to give herself to one man wholeheartedly. She chooses in obedience to live her marriage vows, to serve her family, to submit herself to Christ in the person of her husband.

A wife and mother's service to her husband and family is

unquestionably sacrificial, for it is unquestionably Christian. In radical contradiction to the ethos of the world, the Christian woman is called to root out any disposition that causes her to ask "What about me?" She is called to value things, not in the light of her rights, but rather in sacrificial love. Christ never spoke of rights, but only of sacrifice, of giving. And since it is better to give than receive, Christian homemaking should be seen by all Catholics as a privileged vocation that is purely sacrificial and purely dedicated to Christ.

The Christian patriarch is well advised to bring his wife flowers both real and metaphorical, for the homemaker's life is not without its drudgery, though that drudgery be sweet and conducive to sanctification. The home is not a Garden of Eden; indeed it is often a Garden of Gethsemane. But although not an earthly paradise, it is nonetheless a foretaste of Heaven. Yes, the Christian homemaker confounds the world. Her values are Christ's, and like Him she contradicts and witnesses to the world. It is the Christian patriarch's duty to both promote those values and keep at bay that world.

The *Ecclesia Domestica*

Ecclesia Domestica translates from Latin as "the house church." The house or domestic church is the family unit. Such a church unit must have order and a spiritual charism. The domestic church of Christian patriarchal families strives to live an order and charism based on the most traditional precepts of the Catholic Faith; this order is Christian patriarchy, and this charism is the seeking of holiness. Holiness initially entails a "setting apart" from the profane, both in externals and, most importantly, in the internal disposition of the Christian. In light of the increasing paganization of the popular culture, in externals this will entail a high degree of "counterculturality."

However, there is a limit to how far the Christian patriarchal family can go in externals; yet in the pursuit of personal holiness the exclusion of the profane and of pride is an exercise without end.

Bishop Fulton Sheen often commented that "when the Church is very holy she is attacked from without, when she is not she is attacked from within." This applies likewise to the *Ecclesia Domestica* and the family, and it is also true conversely: to the degree the family is attacked from without, so must its holiness increase. To the degree that the outside world is profane and secular, the home must be proportionally holy and cloistered. And the world of the twenty-first century is profane and secular indeed, Hell-bent on destroying both the family and the Faith.

Hence, these are not the times for the very heart of the Christian home to be divided between such a world and her family. Rather these are times for a woman's exclusive devotion to home and hearth as a complement to Christian Patriarchy. As St. Paul exhorts in Ephesians 5:

> Husbands should love their wives just as Christ loved the Church and sacrificed himself for her to make her holy. He made her clean by washing her in water with a form of words, so that when he took her to himself she would be glorious, with no speck or wrinkle or anything like that, but holy and faultless.

In the Church it is the hidden vocation of monasticism that generates the holiness that keeps evil in check and strengthens those in an active apostolate. Likewise, it is the hidden life of the wife that generates the holiness that inspires and strengthens her family and keeps the world at bay. Destroy the religious life, as heretical reformers, Communists, fascists, and secularists have all attempted, and you destroy the Church. Destroy the exclusive devotion of a woman to the home, and you destroy the family. Although the Church cannot be destroyed, the family can and is being destroyed. Hence this is the time for mothers to dedicate themselves as never before to the sanctification of home life. This is a time that requires nothing less than a woman's complete dedication and exclusive allegiance to the home and family.

The home must be a holy place, a place in which God dwells, a place set apart. In her home a woman must be ever vigilant so that the spirit of the world does not insinuate itself. Her husband, who must be in the world and to some extent is brutalized by it, cannot always be expected to be sensitive to every slight breath of secularity that intrudes upon the home. It is the woman, ever so careful to remain detached from the spirit of the world, who must reside in peace and tranquility, and not succumb to the hectic, frantic commotion that characterizes even homemaking today. A Christian homemaker should strive to lead a contemplative life; that is, a life where prayer permeates all. Such a life is not achieved by her leaving the home for the oratory, but rather by sanctifying her daily chores and offering them up as prayers. It is from the contemplative heart of the Christian wife that the cloistered, holy atmosphere of the home derives.

The Christian homemaker must set the rhythm of her home in contradistinction to the rhythm of the world, calming down those that come from outside, and helping them rid themselves of the spirit of the world. All members of the family should hold the home as a sacred place. In order to facilitate such an attitude, it is an edifying domestic practice to have those arriving from outside stop at the threshold and bless themselves from the holy water font, praying God to cast off the spirit of the world as they do so.

The rhythm of the Christian home should be conducive to the simple appreciation of life, its sorrows and joys—the tears of child, the gurgling of an infant—so often passed over in the rush of the world. The small, simple things must be appreciated and savored, for it is they that make up the most precious part of human life, and it is toward them that the domestic arts are ordered. In such a home the Christian patriarch finds both the reason for his battles and the refreshment from them.

A Christian patriarch, then, is well advised to follow the old Catholic adage to choose a girl to be his bride who is *home-loving*. For to develop this rhythm of the home, a Christian woman must be home-loving, and as such, anchor her family to the home as well.[44] She must guard against the disruption of frequent forays into the world. Although such outings are often necessitated, she must, nonetheless, be strict in discerning the parameters of necessity. Even homeschooling families may find themselves hardly ever home: too many events and opportunities, and no one wants to be left out or have their children left out. Discerning opportunities with the *spirit of poverty* will facilitate prudence in this regard: one needn't do it all, or even most of it, or at times any of it. So too, weekends should not be characterized by an increased level of mobility, for family outings or long drives. Weekends are the time of Sabbath, of rest and quiet. They are also a time of work no doubt (though doing nothing but the essentials on a Sunday), but work done around the home and with each other; and of fun too, but a fun that is again found in being together in and around the home: daughters and mother baking, sons and father building, a game of cards or ball, a time for heart-to-heart talks, and a time for prayer. Sundays should be especially distinguished: maybe by a

---

44. "The wife should love to remain at home, unless compelled by necessity to go out; and she should never presume to leave home without her husband's consent." (*Catechism of Trent on the Duties of the Wife*)

special after-Mass Sunday brunch (and subsequent naps!), or a Sunday dinner with a special desert. But regardless of the particulars of a weekend (or vacation time for that matter), recreation, relaxation, and refreshment should be found primarily in the home.

The Woman's Witness to the World

In the past it was the religious who were the radical witness to the world of the Christian Faith. They were an eschatological sign, a sign of the way things were before the Fall, a sign to the way things should be, and a sign of the way things will be after this world passes away. But that was in a Christian society. Though the religious life is still the highest of callings and though their lives of prayer and service are essential to the Church, religious Brothers and Sisters are utterly beyond the comprehension of the modern, secular mentality.

Today it is not the celibate that confounds the world, but the faithful, Christian, married couple that is fully open to life, neither contracepting nor having a contraceptive mentality. Today it is not the religious vow of obedience that shocks the world, but the obedience and submission of a wife to her husband, of children to their parents, of a man to Christ and His Church. It is not the poverty of monasticism that shocks the world's economic sensibilities, but rather the large, one-income family. Today it is not the garb of nuns that witnesses to feminine grace and modesty, but the Christian woman in her full-flowing skirt or in her mantilla at Mass. It is not the devotions of the monk that leave today's world dumbstruck, but rather the devotion of the Christian man to his wife and family. It is the Christian family that confronts today's world with Christ, and it is most readily the Christian woman who, like the holy, consecrated virgins of the past, gives eloquent witness to the transcendent values of the Faith. Indeed, the religious of the past were much less a stumbling block to their Christian culture than Christian women are today to their secular culture. Christian patriarchs must prayerfully protect and lovingly encourage their wives and daughters as these women meekly accept their countercultural role, helping them peacefully transcend the stares of the world and keep their eyes on Christ.

When choosing a bride for his patriarchal family, a man must transcend the worldly valuation of womanhood by choosing a woman who has chosen Christ. Like a woman that seeks perfection in the cloister, this complementary wife-to-be of the Christian patriarch should be "poor in spirit," truly renouncing the things of the world (be they outside employment or unnecessary outings to the mall). She should be chaste and virginal in her exclusive love and devotion to her future husband and Christ. She should be modest and reserved in dress and comportment. She should reject the phantasms of "romance" (proffered in soap operas and paperback novels) and the general obscenity of the mass media and worldly culture. She too must be obedient and submissive: renouncing her will, her rights, her pride. What a priceless gift such a woman is! That such a soul is entrusted to the Christian patriarch should be overwhelming indeed, both humbling him in his inherent inadequacy and challenging him to an august sanctity.

Today large families are in themselves witnessing and countercultural. The number of children in a family, of course, is not necessarily indicative of sanctity or Catholicity (though it may be an insidious source of spiritual pride for the parents; to think that the number of children one has is proof of one's sanctity is more akin to Calvinism than Catholicism). But although a large number of children is not the sole criteria for determining the zealousness and Catholicity of a family, it is, at face value, indicative of being open to God's Providence and of following the Church's now radically countercultural teaching on contraception. Procreation is the end of marriage; Scripture says it is also a means by which a woman is saved.[45]

The Art of Christian Homemaking

The Christian patriarch must do all he can to facilitate his wife's special duty of homemaking, for the application of its domestic arts is essential to the development of a pervasive Christian ambiance in the home and the subsequent training of children in virtue. The spirit of homemaking is that of poverty, simplicity, and self-sufficiency. It rejects consumerism, commercialism, and mass production.

The domestic arts are the human-sized, quiet skills conducive to contemplation and prayer and aimed at self-sufficiency, and include such diverse activities as cooking, baking, subsistence gardening, sewing and needle-work, canning, and the practice of conventional and alternative medicine. And homemaking is indeed an art. Until the ascendancy of feminism in the late sixties, home economics was an accepted academic field, with many a college offering it as a degree major. And homemaking is indeed a highly crucial art. Food preparation, for instance, is not only essential for health but is an integral part of an authentic Catholic culture. The Church's very designation of its holy days as "feast days" demarcates the importance that meals have.

For a woman (and her daughters) to spend a day in the kitchen preparing for that feast day meal is a noble and pious task. Indeed, even the daily breaking of bread together is nothing less than a domestic sacramental. The family meal, especially the evening meal, is the central event of domestic life. It is a

---

45. Cf. 1 Tim. 2:15

time of family prayer (that should always be "prayerful" regardless of the urgency of hunger) and a time of familial formality. Polite, high-minded discussion, as well as polite table manners, should be cultivated. Conversational topics, properly under the tutorial guidance of the father, should be of an edifying nature for all. Gossip should be absolutely barred, and a father may well consider a lesson he would like to convey during the meal.

But, as with many of the domestic arts in the consumer age, the culinary arts are becoming lost arts, and the quiet family repast a thing of the past. With the onslaught of fast, prepackaged, and processed foods, and a mentality geared toward convenience, the family meal, properly one of the most intimate of times, has become commercialized and mass marketed, as well as unhealthy. Just as Western culture has become profanely tasteless in music and theater, so too has it become tasteless in the culinary arts. Just as the ear, eye, and critical sensibilities can be brutalized by the uncouth and profane; so too can the palate, digestive system, and nutritional health be brutalized.

Since homemaking's domestic and culinary arts are lost arts, the Christian woman must rediscover them, teaching her own daughters in the process. From the time they can mix a bowl, little girls should be incorporated into the kitchen routine. Though at first it would be easier if they were anywhere but in the kitchen, in the end the dividends will pay off splendidly. The little girl's place, just like the mother's, is in and around the home; she must learn to be home-loving. A mother should be especially close to her daughter. Unlike a mother's relation with a son that could hamper the necessary "cutting of the apron strings," a mother is singularly blessed in her relationship with her daughter, in which she can and should be her daughter's best friend, her womanly confidant.

A homemaker must not only discover the lost arts of

homemaking, but the art of being a Christian lady as well. Once again, the Catechism of Trent summarizes the comportment of the Christian lady:

> Let not their adorning be the outward plaiting of the hair, or the wearing of gold, or the putting on of apparel: but the hidden man of the heart in the incorruptibility of a quiet and meek spirit, which is rich in the sight of God. For after this manner heretofore the holy women also, who trusted in God, adorned themselves, being in subjection to their own husbands, as Sarah obeyed Abraham, calling him lord.

Yet developing standards of modest dress and comportment, of recreational activities, and of entertainment, to name a few, remains to some extent partly an inexact process. This process is inexact because it is an aspect of creating Catholic culture, that is, of enculturating the Faith. With few role models to turn to, Catholic women today should themselves ever seek new standards of Catholic womanhood. Though such standards are new, they should be second to none that have preceded them, distilling all that was edifying from the past and applying them in an uncompromising manifestation of Christian womanhood. In order for them to do so they must have recourse to the Blessed Mother as a guide in womanly deportment, modesty, and spirit. A woman who knows the Blessed Mother, who has her as *her* closest confidant and friend, will be able to answer the many questions of deportment and modesty that arise: "Would Our Lady wear such an outfit?" "Would she engage in such conversations?" "Would she partake of such entertainment?" And far be from the mind of the Christian patriarch to seek to limit his wife or daughters in their conformity to the Blessed Virgin Mary. May he ever help his spouse and daughters to become *truly ladylike, like Our Lady!*

The Harmony of Hierarchy

As previously mentioned, among orthodox and zealous Catholics familial matriarchy (at least in spiritual and moral matters) is the rule. Such a phenomenon both countermands God's law and eviscerates the Faith; it is the very reason Catholicism remains so ineffectual in combating the secular forces arrayed against it.

Even if a woman gives lip-service to the ideals of patriarchy, she must be on guard against actions that speak louder than her words. Does a wife shrilly countermand a valid decision of her husband? Then she sins against the domestic order. Does she allow herself to aggressively vent angry feelings of vexation or disagreement with him? Then she sins against submission. Does she allow a spirit of pride or obstinacy to well up and be displayed in behavior or words, even if ever so subtly, when she feels her husband has made a poor decision? Then she sins against obedience. Does she take undue satisfaction in proving her point, or being in the right when her husband makes a mistake? Then she sins against love and honor. Does she do any of the above in front of her children? Then she compounds her sin with the sin of scandal, for her children subconsciously take to heart every word, action, attitude, and nuance of hers, which then germinate in their hearts until they sprout magnified in their own behavior.

Again from the Catechism of the Council of Trent:

> [I]n this the conjugal union chiefly consists, let wives never forget that next to God they are to love their husbands, to esteem them above all others, yielding to them in all things not inconsistent with Christian piety, a willing and ready obedience.

Thus that which would be considered insubordinate behavior

toward a boss in the workplace is surely not acceptable behavior towards one's husband, who is the one a wife must love and honor *next to God alone*. Unfortunately, the old maxim "familiarity breeds contempt" seems to hold true. A wife must, therefore, be ever on guard against showing even the slightest signs of contempt. The best way to do so is by seeing her husband as Christ, by submitting herself to him with nothing short of a religious obedience. A pious nun, when faced with a disagreeable or even absurd order from her superior, obeys without question or demur, for in doing so she mortifies her pride and will, and gets about her primary task of sanctification. Yes, this places a great burden upon a wife, whose vocation best suits her to "turn the other cheek," as opposed to those who are in the world. But this does not mean she is a "doormat," for she will not facilitate evil and would rather be rejected by an erring husband than condone his sin. It is this desire to facilitate not evil but rather holiness that is the very reason a wife seeks not to return anger for anger or spite for spite. Of course, optimally it is the reciprocal combination of a husband's love and devotion and a wife's submission and obedience that sanctifies both in holy Matrimony.

Even when a husband's command or decision is less than optimal, though not immoral, it should be followed, at least until there is an appropriate time to consult with him. That appropriate time is hardly ever in front of the children. A mother knows her children better than does a father, and should even have more common sense in making everyday decisions for them, but she does greater harm than good to them if she is in the habit of countermanding her husband when he is at home and properly exercising his office as head of the family. A wife must make a point of showing deferment and docility to her husband in front of her children, just as she makes a point in showing them other pious or proper modes of behavior and attitudes. To quote again Pope Pius XII's exhortation to newly-wed wives:

> And do you, O brides, lift up your hearts. Do not be content merely to accept, and—one might almost say—to tolerate this authority of your husbands, to whom God has subjected you according to the dispositions of nature and of grace; in your sincere submission you must love that authority and love it with the same respectful love you bear towards the authority of Our Lord Himself from Whom all authority flows.[46]

A Christian husband's greatest earthly blessing is a wise and insightful wife. Such a wife facilitates her husband's headship by being humble and submissive so that her suggestions and advice cannot be construed as challenges to the husband's authority. Truly, the establishment of patriarchal hierarchy facilitates the free exchange of ideas and opinions between man and wife, for there is no threat or intent of usurpation. And it is a blessed and wise husband who takes full advantage of his wife's insights into the affairs of the family.

A good wife, like a good follower, is one who facilitates her husband's leadership. A good wife does not lack initiative; for passivity is not the result of an authentic submissiveness. Rather, receptivity goes hand-in-hand with submissiveness. Where a passive wife's heart will lie fallow, a truly submissive and receptive wife will take her husband's vision to heart, nurture it, cultivate it, and bring it to fruition. As mirrored in the intimate act of marital love, creation depends on womanly submission and receptivity to manly initiative and giving. Again, it is a husband's superlative and unique devotion to his wife that best facilitates this spirit of submission.

---

46. Pius XII, *Allocution to Newly-Weds.*, para. 82.

Womanly love is inherently nurturing and maternal, and no less so when it is love of a husband. A man should be able to draw on the refreshing springs of his wife's maternal heart without fear of diminishing his authority. The patriarchal order does not exclude the nurturing of a wife for her husband, nor does such a nurturing in any way diminish the patriarchal authority. Rather, a wife's nurturing love for her husband specifically strengthens him in his manhood and his patriarchal office, for she is his particular source of grace and love.

The Cause of Catholic Community

It is true that Catholic families aren't meant to be subsumed under any communal rule save the rule of the Church. It is true that husbands and wives aren't meant to be separated in their spiritual lives. It is true that it is the husband that is the absolute head of his family, and no organization or person may properly supplant or interfere with that headship. Yet Catholic families do need other families. The Faith is communal, and the family, though it is the fundamental political entity, is an incomplete political entity. Thus, for that commitment and that order to be fully efficacious, small communities of families who share a commitment to Christ and the domestic patriarchal order must be formed.

If Catholic communities are based on the common denominator of patriarchal hierarchy, then any danger of supplanting the family with extraneous structures of authority will be avoided. If men as brothers in Christ gather together based on the specific principle of familial hierarchy then all their efforts will be properly ordered toward the family. Truly, this uniting of men as brothers in Christ is not an option, for it is they collectively who must lead the community as a whole. Men of these days must learn to bond as brothers, must learn even

how to be men on the natural level, before they can learn how
to be Christian patriarchs; hence the need for fraternal organizations to foster this brotherhood, manhood, and patriarchy.
Wives should be well aware of the difficult task that lies before
their husbands, and thus encourage them and not begrudge
them the fraternal support needed to learn and carry out the
duties of the Christian patriarch; for the Christian patriarch has
the most arduous task both in personal growth and leadership
of the family and the community. If husbands are fraternally
united, their wives will become sisters as a matter of course,
for it is inherent in their feminine nature to bond as women.

Again, any patriarchal fraternal organization must have as
its end not its own existence but rather the strengthening of
the familial patriarchal order and the community of patriarchal
families. Such an organization should be based on clearly stated
Christian principles, such as those gathered together from the
Church in this book. Men need to see the principles and ideals
in black and white and then be challenged to live up to them.

Fathers must then apply these Christian patriarchal principles and set the standards of adherence. In this the specifics of
the particular familial and community makeup requires varied
degrees and pace in the implementation of Catholic patriarchal
principles. In this regard, it is wise for the Christian familial
patriarch to govern so as to *gently prod his family toward virtue* as he
seeks to again heed St. Augustine's exhortation to the familial
patriarchs of his diocese, his "fellow bishops":

> Each and every one of you have in the home the bishop's
> office to see to it that neither his wife nor his son nor his
> daughter nor even his servant fall away from the truth. For
> they were bought with a great price.

Today the perils of "falling away from the truth" are graver
than ever before. It is a small minority of Catholics who assent

fully to Church teaching on faith and morals, who recognize their own sinfulness and the accelerating profanity of the world and seek to compromise less with that sinfulness and that world as they conform themselves more to "Christ and Him crucified." Yet it is these families[47] who will be the beginnings of a new Christian patriarchy, of new communities of Catholic patriarchal families, and hence a new Christendom.

Yes, the Catholic family is under a vicious and devastating attack. Hence the absolute need for the formation of a deeply bonded family under the sure and inspired command of its God-ordained patriarchal captain. Such a familial patriarchal bond must be deep and pure, a charitable bond in Christ, a sacramental bond of holy Matrimony, a bond forged in the travails of the Cross and cured in the light of the Resurrection. In conjunction with other such families, these new Christian patriarchal families so bonded and so imbued will, by the abundant grace of God, produce the Catholic communities, the Catholic culture, and the Catholic saints able to steadfastly withstand and heroically witness to the world today.

---

47. Although the ideals of Christian patriarchy may best resonate with this last segment of Catholics, they are also edifying, encouraging, and challenging for those less militant in their faith. Nonetheless, the acceptance of the teaching of familial Christian patriarchy will itself prove a Rubicon that separates the zealous from the lukewarm, the Christ-like from the complacent and comfort-seeking, the orthodox from the heterodox, indeed, the militant Christian men from the compromising boys. This demarcation goes as well for the women who have chosen piously to follow their husbands in Christ.

Appendix A

Pope John Paul II and "Mutual Submission"

THE FOLLOWING is a study of His Holiness John Paul II's[48] writings as they touch on the patriarchal hierarchy of the family. More aptly it is a study of the late Pope's writings as a private theologian, since most of them under consideration here were written before his election to the papacy in 1978. The intent of this study is to examine whether certain innovative and, as such, controversial aspects of these writings can be located within the corpus of magisterial teachings on familial patriarchy; that is, to attempt to position them for possible integration as a legitimate development of doctrine. Indeed, it is this sort of integration that will give rise to the further development of the doctrine of Christian patriarchy.

At the outset it must be recognized that there is no charism inherent in the papal office that would *guarantee* that all theologically progressive utterances of a Pope are in fact a valid development of doctrine. In the present case, any development of the doctrine of Christian familial patriarchy must *leave intact the singular headship of the Christian husband and father* to have the possibility of being a legitimate development of this doctrine.

---

48. Even though most of the writings cited herein were written by Karol Wojtyla as a private theologian before his ascendency to the papacy, his pontifical name is respectfully used throughout.

Ephesians 5:21-33 and "Mutual Submission"

His Holiness Pope John Paul II used his Wednesday catechesis audiences to read much of his private theological works, among them *The Theology of Marriage and Celibacy*. In this work, he introduces the novel concept of "mutual submission" in his exegesis of Ephesians 5.[49] The scriptural passage reads:

> Being subject one to another, in the fear of Christ. Let women be subject to their husbands, as to the Lord: Because the husband is the head of the wife, as Christ is the head of the church.[50]

John Paul II takes the first sentence, which at face value simply gives the ultimate reason why one is to be submissive, and gives it a specific prescriptive meaning: "The author speaks of mutual subjection of the spouses, husband and wife, and in this way explains the words which he will write afterward on the subjection of the wife to the husband."[51] From this first premise, John Paul II deduces that "the husband and wife are in fact 'subject to one another,' and are mutually subordinate to one another." Furthermore, he states, "Love makes the husband simultaneously subject to the wife, and thereby subject to the Lord Himself, *just as* the wife to the husband"[52] [*emphasis mine*]. This novel premise of "mutual submission" is properly viewed as an *interpretation* rather than as a translation of the passage; for the author of Ephesians does not explicitly "speak of mutual submission of the spouses," nor does this concept appear in the rest of Holy Scripture or any previous magisterial or authoritative exegesis of this passage.

---

49. See Chapter two for the traditional exegesis of this passage.
50. Eph. 5:21-23.
51. John Paul II, General Audience, *Catechesis on Marriage and Celibacy in the Light of the Resurrection of the Body* (11 August 1982) sec. 3.
52. *Ibid.*, sec. 4.

To construe the interpretative concept of "mutual sub-mission" as a development of doctrine (that is, as an integral growth from, and harmonious with, previous Church teach-ings and exegesis) requires an expanded understanding of the word "submission." It is true that a husband, in a certain sense, submits himself to his wife by giving his life for her; however this broadening of the term has never been employed by the Church in her exegesis of the Ephesians 5 or her teaching on marriage. Broadening "submission" in this way gives the term an analogous meaning: it cannot be applied exactly the same to both husband and wife, but only in a somewhat similar manner. This analogous broadening of the term is necessary to keep intact its previously understood meaning—that of a hierarchi-cal order—and thus permit it to be incorporated into the cor-pus of authentic Church teachings. An orthodox construction, then, requires that John Paul II's "mutual submission of the spouses" be seen as an analogous submission, where the man paradoxically submits himself to a life of authority that entails both headship and sacrificial service.

Elsewhere in this exegesis of Ephesians 5, John Paul II asserts that by the passage " 'wives, be subject to your hus-bands, as to the Lord' . . . the author does not intend to say that the husband is the 'lord' of the wife."

For this statement to be construed as harmonious with pre-vious Church teachings on the subject, "lord" must be under-stood in a strictly pejorative sense; that is, as a "lording over" abuse of authority or, as John Paul II says in the same passage, an understanding of a husband's lordly position as "a one-sided domination."[53] But the other meaning of "lord," the positive

---

53. This pejorative use of "lord," in the sense of "lording over," can be seen in the writings of Hans Urs von Balthasar, a favored theologian of John Paul II's, on the papacy. Balthasar's ardent intent, nonetheless, is to preserve and strengthen authentic papal authority.

meaning, must not thereby be seen as discarded, for the husband as "lord of the wife" is not only intrinsic to the Church's teachings on familial hierarchy, but also in accord with the most fundamental principle of biblical exegesis. This first exegetical principle is to interpret scriptural passages in light of other similar writings of the day, most especially companion scriptural writings. In the epistle of St. Peter, Christian wives are exhorted to imitate the "holy women of the past . . . like Sarah, who was obedient to Abraham, and called him her *lord.*"[54] So too, the rest of the Pauline letters continually stress patriarchal hierarchy.[55]

It is the clause, "give way to one another in the Lord" at the beginning of the Ephesians passage that John Paul II uses as the cornerstone of his novel exegesis of Ephesians 5. Yet to construe "give way to one another in the Lord" as a universal prescription of mutual, univocal submission would, in effect, do away with all hierarchical order, including that of the parents and children, Magisterium and faithful, and government and citizens. Instead, a reading of the entire passage in accord with simple, grammatical logic clearly shows that "give way to one another in the Lord" indicates both the source of legitimate authority and the spirit of dutiful submission. The author of Ephesians goes on to delineate some specific domestic relationships of authority and submission that find their source and spirit in the Lord, beginning with that which is the model for the rest, the relation of man and wife. If John Paul II's use of the term "mutual submission" were to be taken in a univocal sense, and hence isolated from previous Church exegesis of the passage, then it would follow that not only is a man to submit to his wife, but, as Ephesians goes on to delineate domestic relations, parents are to submit to their children as well.

---

54. 1 Pet. 3:5-6
55. Cf. 1 Cor. 7:1-7; 11:1-16; 14:33-38; Eph. 5:21-33; Col. 3:18-21; 1 Tim. 2:8-15; Titus 2:1-10

If the term "submission" is construed in an implicit, secondary manner that includes a man's—or a parent's—giving of his life in sacrificial service of those under his authority, then the explicit, primary meaning, which entails a hierarchical family structure, remains intact. This primary, explicit meaning, the meaning previously asserted by the Church, is that which is derived from a simple reading of the passage.

John Paul II's Purifying of Hierarchy

Publishing as Pope, John Paul II's most authoritative pronouncement to date on the issue of familial hierarchy, found in the apostolic letter *Mulieris Dignitatem*, contains a puzzling passage that employs a historical-critical methodology in its exegesis and seems to equate familial patriarchy with slavery:

> The awareness that in marriage there is mutual "subjection of the spouses out of reverence for Christ," and not just that of the wife to the husband, must gradually establish itself in hearts, consciences, behavior and customs. St. Paul not only wrote: "In Christ Jesus . . . there is no more man or woman," but also wrote: "There is no more slave or freeman." Yet how many generations were needed for such a principle to be realized in the history of humanity through the abolition of slavery![56]

Here, as elsewhere in his papal pronouncements, John Paul II uses his private writings as a basis and reference; he premises his argument on the principal that in marriage there is "mutual submission of the spouses." Elsewhere in the passage the use of quotation marks refers to a direct quotation of a scriptural

---

56. John Paul II, apostolic letter, *Mulieris Dignitatem*, (15 August 1988) Ch. VI, Sec. 24.

passage, yet here they are not enclosing a scriptural quotation but rather a highly interpretative extrapolation of a scriptural passage. It is important to keep in mind that "mutual subjection of the spouses" is not a given scriptural or doctrinal premise, but rather a concept that comes from John Paul II's prior writings as a private theologian.

Use of this principle of "mutual submission" has led some to believe that John Paul II has circumvented or even negated the Church's traditional exegesis of Ephesians 5 and the derived teaching on the patriarchal hierarchy of the family. But again, in keeping with the intent of viewing the writings in harmony with previous teachings, the concept of mutual submission must be seen as making way for the promotion of an authentic Christian patriarchy based on the kingly, yet sacrificial model of Christ, or at least not implying any diminishment of the doctrine of familial patriarchal authority. So too, his comparison of the state of wifely submission to that of slavery must be viewed as a desire to do away with a worldly or pagan patriarchy of brute dominance, while promoting an authentic Christian patriarchy based solely on the commission of Christ. Such a development purifies and defines the unique nature of Christian authority and patriarchy; it does not do away with it, but rather elevates it.

John Paul II's Reconstruction and Reinterpretation of Ephesians 5

It is not possible, nor licit, nor even desirable, to discount the entirety of Ephesians 5 as non-essential, or to delete it, as is being illicitly done in the readings in some parishes and dioceses. For this same passage is the primary scriptural basis for the ecclesiological doctrine that Christ is the head of the Church and that the Church is His bride. In addition, this passage provides the primary scriptural basis for the doctrine of the unity and singularity of the Church, as well as the matrimonial principle of exclusivity. However, in his private theological work *Catechesis on Marriage and Celibacy*, John Paul II downplays Ephesians 5's essential theme of patriarchal hierarchy of the family in an effort to eliminate any abusive use of the passage to justify male brute domination. Therefore, in order to keep intact the ecclesiology and marital theology, while at the same time attempting to remedy any misuse of Ephesians 5, John Paul II mutes the patriarchal theme by vigorously reworking the passage.

This exegetical re-vamping is based on the extra-textual assumption that the ecclesiastical/familial analogy is used not to show how the relationship of man and wife is a reflection of the spiritual union of Christ and the Church, but rather as a sort of parable of the time, employing that culture's experience of marriage to illuminate the relationship of Christ and the Church. John Paul II advances that in order to properly understand Ephesians 5:21, the text must be read in a reverse manner ("to re-read the analogy inversely") than which it is written and that this reworking of the text is the "normative" reading that renders the primary meaning ("to express first of all") of the passage:

> Marriage corresponds to the vocation of Christians as spouses only if, precisely, that love is reflected and effected therein. This will become clear if we attempt to reread the Pauline analogy inversely, that is, beginning with the relationship of Christ to the Church and turning next to the relationship of husband and wife in marriage.
> . . . We can presume that the author, who has already explained that the submission of the wife to the husband as head is intended as reciprocal submission "out of reverence for Christ," goes back to the concept rooted in the mentality

of the time, to express first of all the truth concerning the
relationship of Christ to the Church . . . [57]

John Paul II here seems to conclude that the author of
Ephesians was not elucidating primarily upon the relationship
of man and wife, but upon that of the Church and Christ, and
that the headship of the man and submission of the wife were
merely accidental examples; examples that today are passé due
to their cultural basis.[58] By proposing that the analogy *is not to
be read analogously* unless we first re-read it inversely, and that
such an inversion's focus on Christ and the Church is what the
author desired "to express first of all," John Paul II is able to
turn the passage into an ecclesiastical statement primarily, while
relegating its domestic prescription to an accidental status.

Still, it must be noted that "the mentality of the times" was
not tending toward patriarchy, but quite the opposite.[59] In fact,
the many exhortations in the epistles concerning patriarchal
familial and ecclesiastical hierarchy were necessitated by the
feminism of the times, especially among the upper class in cos-
mopolitan Roman cities or colonies such as Ephesus. (Recall
from chapter two how Pope Pius XII characterized the domestic disintegration of the ancient world.)

The Typification of Ephesians 5

John Paul II's re-construction of Ephesians 5:21 is accomplished by changing the literary device used by St. Paul from
that of typification to that of parable. Typification is a literary device that shows how essential characteristics and internal
relations of a subtype are derived from a prototype. Parable is

---

57. John Paul II, *Catechesis on Marriage and Celibacy;* sec. 3, 4, 5.
58. *Ibid.*, sec. 6.
59. See Chapter 2, "Ancient Paganism."

a literary device used to illustrate a sublime truth by comparing it to a common occurrence. Typification is used to bring out a truth about the more mundane concept, in the case of Ephesians 5:21 the truth of the domestic order. Parable, however, is used to illuminate the more sublime concept, which in John Paul II's reconstruction is the relation of Christ and the Church. By changing the literary device of the passage from that of typification to that of parable, John Paul II is thus able to render the passage a discourse on ecclesiology rather than on domestic relations.

Yet the Church has always taught that marriage is modeled on Christ's relationship with the Church. Indeed the sacramentality of marriage is due to its being a type of the union of Christ and His Church. That is, marriage as type derives or patterns its character and internal dynamics from the prototype, Christ and the Church. Marriage as type is temporal; Christ's relation with the Church as prototype is eternal, not only lasting beyond marriage but somehow preceding it as well. That is why St. Paul can imply that the union of man and wife as it was in the pre-fallen state, where a man leaves his father and mother and becomes one flesh with his wife, is because of the pre-existing prototype of Christ and the Church. The Church has always considered the Ephesians 5:21 passage as one that typifies the relation of husband and wife in accord with the prototype relation of Christ and the Church:

> In His most far-reaching foresight God thus decreed that husband and wife should be the natural beginning of the human race. [Footnoted as follows:] As fact and as symbol, nothing could be more beautiful and significant than this act of God. It is all a marvel of His love, *the climax of which is reached in the institution of Matrimony, imaging the mystical nuptials of Christ with His Bride*, the Church, taken from His own open

side in His sleep of death upon the Cross. In that union of Christ with His Church we have for all time the model of every Christian marriage.[60] [*Emphasis mine*].

Finally, St. Thomas says, "a type is a protestation of the truth, and therefore can never be detracted from in the slightest degree."

In addition, the reading of Ephesians 5:21 as a typification—meant to bring out a truth about the marital relationship by deriving that truth from the illustration of Christ's relation with the Church—is warranted by the context of the rest of the chapter, which is clearly a treatise on proper Christian behavior, both personal and domestic, as opposed to a treatise on ecclesiology. This typification does not, however, diminish the ecclesiological import of the passage. Unlike the literary device of parable, in which the mundane illustration is poetical and is not intended to convey a truth about itself (for example, the parable of the laborers in the vineyard[61] is not intended as an economic statement on just wages), the use of typification necessarily asserts the higher truth of the illustrated prototype.

John Paul II further seeks to transform Ephesians 5 by the statement that the author of Ephesians "has already explained that the submission of the wife to the husband as head is intended as reciprocal submission 'out of reverence for Christ.'" This imputes a meaning to the phrase "submit to one another out of reverence for Christ'" that is manifestly *not* explained by St. Paul in the extended manner subsequently developed by John Paul II.

If the late Pope's novel extrapolation of "submit to one another out of reverence for Christ" is not to be viewed as deriving from a premise that is totally outside the context of

---

60. Leo XIII, *Arcanum*, encyclical, 1880.
61. Matt. 20:1-16

either Scripture or Sacred Tradition, it must be interpreted in the context of not only the rest of the passage but the other Pauline and Petrine epistles as well. It thus must be considered to be in harmony with the traditional teaching on familial patriarchy, regardless of its lack of reiteration of that teaching, and intended only to eliminate that which is a distortion of that teaching—a male brute and pagan dominance. Nor, it must confidently be supposed, does John Paul II's characterization of the passage as "rooted in the mentality of the times" reflect an intent to implement the historical-critical method in an effort to deconstruct and eliminate one of the Church's constant teachings.

Genesis 3:16 and Preternatural Hierarchy

In *Mulieris Dignitatem*, section 10, Pope John Paul II refers to one of the consequences of original sin: "thou shalt be under thy husband's power, and he shall have dominion over thee."[62] The Holy Father writes:

> This domination indicates the disturbance and loss of the stability of that fundamental equality which the man and the women possess in the unity of the two . . . The matrimonial union requires respect for and a perfecting of the true personal subjectivity of both of them. The woman cannot become the object of domination and male possession . . . The words of the Book of Genesis quoted previously (3:16) show how . . . the inclination to sin will burden the mutual relationship of man and woman.

Here, neither the assertion of fundamental equality, nor the condemnation of woman as "an object of domination and a

---

62. Gen. 3:16.

male possession," is contrary to authentic Christian patriarchy. The former is but the assertion of the equal dignity of men and women, the latter is but the condemnation of a pagan or worldly patriarchal order based on power.

Yet in the same section in *Mulieris Dignitatem*, John Paul II's use of phrases such as "fundamental equality" and "a unity of two . . . called to exist mutually one for the other," are liable to be construed as implying that before the Fall there was no hierarchical order:

> *These words of Genesis* [3:16] refer directly to marriage, but indirectly *they concern the different spheres of social life:* the situations in which the woman remains disadvantaged or discriminated against by the fact of being a woman. The revealed truth concerning the creation of the human being as male and female [i.e. as fundamentally equal before the Fall] constitutes the principle argument against all the objectively injurious and unjust situations which contain and express the inheritance of sin."

An example of "injurious and unjust situations" is given in *Familiaris Consortio*: "the oppressive presence of a father, especially where there still prevails the phenomenon of 'machismo,' or a wrong superiority of male prerogative which humiliates women [i.e. "causes psychological and moral imbalance and notable difficulties in family relationships"]."[63] Again, the Holy Father's words, in harmony with constant Church teaching, must be applied to "a wrong superiority" rather than to all patriarchal prerogative. So too, although there was no sin before the Fall and hence no sinful domination, there still existed a patriarchal order.[64] Pope John Paul II's teaching, then, understood in the light of constant Church teaching, advances that Christ

---

63. *Familiaris Consortio* 25
64. See Chapter 2

purified and restored marriage to its pristine but still patriarchal state, eradicating not familial hierarchy but rather that which was a sinful perversion of it.

As a final note on *Mulieris Dignitatem,* it should be mentioned that John Paul II did not intend to convey a dogmatic statement when he wrote "that the first sin is the sin of man, created by God male and female. It is also the sin of the 'first parents,' to which is connected its hereditary character. In this sense we call it 'original sin.'"[65] For though the first sin was that of Eve, it was the second sin of Adam, as head of the human race, which was original sin. If only Eve had sinned, there would have been no original sin nor Fall. The pivotal dogmatic teaching on original sin states that it was through Adam exclusively that humanity inherited its consequences. In light of the dogma of original sin as committed and transmitted exclusively by Adam, it is irrefutable that Adam in his preternatural state had a most august and crucial headship that was not found in Eve.

Restoring Preternatural Hierarchy

Christ indeed came to restore the dignity and loftiness of marriage to its preternatural state, and came indeed to elevate it above that state. But that restored and elevated state was not one of non-hierarchical equality but rather a patriarchal hierarchy based on the very authority of Christ. Christ's restoration of marriage, then, entails not the elimination of the patriarchal hierarchy of the family, but rather its elevation from a sinful, worldly context: which is exactly what St. Paul and all subsequent positive magisterial pronouncements on the subject have strongly affirmed.

Furthermore, the consequences of original sin have not

---

65. *Mulieris Dignitatem* 9

traditionally been considered sinful in themselves, nor results of an inclination to sin, but rather as embodying "remedies that limit the damaging effects of sin."[66] Christ did not do away with the effects of original sin, but rather made them the very means of man's sanctification (consider the redemptive nature of suffering through childbirth and manual labor). So although the punishments prescribed in Genesis do not give husbands a license for sinful domination, they do establish a woman's need ("desire" or "yearning") for her husband and a husband's ruling position. It is the disorder of sin that necessitates that ruling, the act of "making straight," be an integral part of headship.

That which is prescribed in Genesis as a result of the Fall may be to some extent alleviated (though not to a degree that they no longer act as "remedies that limit the damaging effects of sin"), but there should be no attempt to circumvent or do away with them, since they were divinely ordained.

Toward A More Authentic Christian Patriarchy

In the same manner as those who feel free to delete from the Deposit of Faith any teaching that was not repeated in the documents of Vatican II (which is the vast majority of Church teaching) by claiming that exclusion is rescission, there are those who wish to discard the traditional teaching of the Church on familial patriarchy due to John Paul II's non-reiteration of that teaching. But non-reiteration is neither rescission nor repudiation. When John Paul II's writings on patriarchy are subsumed as best they can be under previous definitive magisterial pronouncements on the subject, what must be gleaned from them is the call for eradication of that which in the past has masqueraded as a Christian patriarchy—not Christian patriarchy itself.

---

66. *Catechism of the Catholic Church*, para. 1609.

Indeed, John Paul II's arguably favorite theologian,[67] the incredibly prolific but at times highly controversial Hans Urs von Balthasar (1905-1988), expressed a similar dynamic as occurring within the papacy itself, which though "purified" nonetheless keeps its authority intact:

> In this official role of the "self-effacing," "unworthy servant" who "only does his duty" and expects no thanks for it,[68] Peter becomes the prototype . . . This *renunciation* which lies at the heart of Catholic office is not primarily an ethical achievement but intrinsic to its structure. The office bearer is bound to exercise an office that is not his own; essentially he directs attention to someone else who "leads him where he does not wish to go"; such an office can only be accepted with "grief"[69] about one's own unworthiness.[70]

Thus, that which can be incorporated into the corpus of Catholic traditional teaching, from the writings of John Paul II on the familial order, can only be that which paves the way for the establishment of a more authentic Christian patriarchy: *a Christian patriarchy unshakable and more authoritative,* being purified of all brutish dominance and worldly power and based solely and firmly on Christ and His commission of authority.

---

67. John Paul II showed his high esteem of Hans Urs von Balthasar when he elected the controversial Swiss priest-theologian, along with Henri De Lubac, to the cardinalate. However, Fr. Balthasar died two days before he was to receive the red hat. (Balthasar's arguably most controversial position was delineated in his self-explanatory titled 1988 monograph, *Dare we hope "that all men be saved"?*)
68. Cf. Luke 17:9-10
69. Cf. John 21:17
70. Balthasar, *op. cit.,* p. 287.

APPENDIX B

The Ideological and Political Assault against Western Patriarchy

IT IS THE anti-Christian ideologies of secularism and liberalism—embodied in the modern state and promoted by the mass media—that have directed the attack upon the traditional familial order. These ideologies, inherently materialistic and therefore at least in practice atheistic, hold that the state is the highest, in fact, the only legitimate authority that exists. As a corollary to what is tantamount to the deification of the state, an absolute code of morality ensues where man is viewed purely as a political being and his good defined exclusively in terms of political rights. And the issuance and bestowal—or rescinding—of these rights are the exclusive domain of the state. It is the state, not God, from which these rights are seen to originate; and it is the state, not man's nature in the image of God, which defines these rights.

The ability to create fundamental rights is the great fulcrum of the secular state. By definition fundamental rights once recognized or declared cannot be altered by legislation. When the state creates a right it creates a moral or political mandate that has the full authority of the law behind it. The secular state's autonomous ability to create legally mandated rights outside the democratic process (in the United States it does so by the decisions of an unelected Supreme Court) renders it omnipotent. This secular creation of rights and their enforcement by law are bound neither by God, nature, nor majority consensus.

The state can thus use legally mandated rights to coercively implement ideological, political, and social agendas with complete political immunity. The ramifications and extension of these rights is limited only by the ability of the state to enforce them. The secular state views its ideology of rights as absolute, and this ideology's ensuing decrees reign tyrannical over every institution in the land, including the church and the family.

The acquiescence of the populace to the dictatorial rise of *state-given* rights, their issuance and legal enforcement, stems from the post-Christian Western world's philosophical and popular belief that rights are the ultimate good and that the assertion of these rights is the highest of virtues. Indeed, in the secular West it is a capital sin to err against rights. Yet even with such a value system firmly established, the masses must be propagandized to accept the creation and imposition of new rights, for every creation of a right takes away a previously established one. Hence the old right must be re-construed as an anti-right; that is, it is seen not as a virtue but as a vice: as a social and political sin that is opposed to sacred state-sanctioned rights.

According to this secular ethos of *state-given* rights there is no greater vice than the practice of patriarchal rights, for there is nothing so grievous as to sin against feminist rights. Feminist rights have been empowered with the greatest degree of social righteousness and political correctness. It is feminism, armed with the power of the state and the propagandizing of the mass media, which has toppled the West's most honored traditions. With its shrill cry of "discrimination," feminism has invaded every segment of society: from the local pub to the national corporation, from the military to the church, from the school to the family. And most telling of all, it is feminism that has dared to claim and win the ultimate right to murder. It is only feminism that has the audacity and power to not only keep this homicidal right, but to increase it despite subsequent, technological imagery and scientific evidence that irrefutably witnesses to both the humanity of the unborn and to the grisly and tortuous murder that is abortion.

The principle of Christian patriarchy directly defies the secular ethos of individual *state-given* rights (as outlined above) and the evil of feminism. Even on a personal level, the assertion of rights often is fueled more by pride than justice. An individual rights-based morality whose dynamic is the promotion of one's own self-interest is opposed to an individual duty-based morality based on the truth that "it is better to give than receive." So too, nothing so contradicts the feminist agenda as the doctrine that states, "wives be submissive and obedient unto your husbands."

In a subtle syntactical distinction, Christian ethics is more concerned with *the right* rather than *rights*. An individual rights-oriented disposition is concerned first and foremost with one's own good. It measures the cost, is concerned as to whether one is receiving as much as one is giving; and is apt to discern that one deserves more than he is getting. In short, it is often fueled by a selfish disposition. But such a disposition, like the concept of rights itself, is not to be found in the gospel message; it is alien to an authentic Christian ethos. Rather that which *is right*, what is just and true and good, is what a Christian must assert. In this sense of *the right*, Christian patriarchy and the men that are called to comprise it have the primary duty and responsibility to preserve, defend, and promote the *rights* of the sacrosanct family and the Church and fight the *wrongs* against it.

Indeed, Christian patriarchal hierarchy is the last bastion against the tyranny of an omnipotent state that has not only usurped the Church's temporal authority and unjustly claimed to be both the arbitrator of what is right and the grantor of rights, but now seeks to finish its coup by usurping the authority that rightly belongs to the family. Having done away with the temporal authority of the Church, the state has but one final obstacle in its assumption of all authority—the obstacle of familial authority. Unwilling to brook any authority outside itself the state senses that familial authority, and most especially patriarchal authority, must be outlawed and destroyed. Hence the state has been waging an unlimited war against this final bastion with a ferocity and success unparalleled in the profane history of Hellish campaigns. The state uses rights, which only it can manufacture and which only it can grant or take away, in its unceasing and systematic bombardment of the family. First the state revoked ancient patriarchal rights and placed in their stead equal rights, thus reconstituting marriage into a contractual democracy of two. But this democracy of two inherently required the intervention of a third party to act as arbitrator. So the state eagerly assumed the role of arbitrator and created its final solution, divorce rights, of which it became the sole grantor.

The state has also used policies and laws of affirmative action as a propaganda tool to entice women out of the home and into the work place, and to force employers to restructure for the admittance of women. This restructuring has doubled the work force, thereby causing wages to be cut in half, and rapidly transformed a one-income economy into a two-income economy. And as of late, the state has launched its disingenuous campaigns against domestic violence and child abuse that take away even basic constitutional rights from parents. Thus the state in its systematic, anti-familial campaign seeks to destabilize the family by dividing man and wife, by outlawing patriarchal authority, by campaigning against the traditional feminine roles of motherhood and homemaking, and by insinuating itself into the inner sanctum of family life.

Why this grand alliance of feminism and state? Without state backing the feminist agenda would have had the most minimal effect on the natural social order. Hence, the feminists depend completely on the state to coercively implement their agenda. And the state finds this feminist agenda to be the perfect weapon in its implicit war against the family. For the state intuits that the family is impenetrable from without if it is united within. And a hierarchical order bequeaths unity as nothing else can. Nothing imbues the family with resiliency and nobility as does patriarchy, where a father takes personal and complete responsibility for his family and a mother dedicates her life exclusively to it. Hence the state eagerly gives *bite* to the feminist's *bark* to "rebel," and the family is breached from within.

And so it is Christian patriarchy that singularly defies the omnipotent state and its exclusive moral currency of rights. It is Christian patriarchy that strikes both at the state and feminism in their unholy alliance. It is Christian patriarchy that confronts and gives battle to the monstrous evil of the day at its most essential level.

The Remote Causes

The rise of nationalism and egalitarianism in the West is looked upon by most as a political advance. But the roots of this rise are found, ominously enough, in the rebellion against the West's universal moral and spiritual authority, the Catholic Church; while its most bitter fruits are the evisceration of the family and the enthronement of the state as an omnipotent authority.

Medieval society was based on an organic concept of societal and familial groups, rather than on individuals. These groups, though unequal in status and privilege, interacted with one another in social harmony. So too, within these groups each member, again admitting of varying degrees of rank, interacted with the others in a harmonious way. And so it was from town, to guild, to the family itself; society was built on harmonious inequality. Individuals were not viewed as independent social entities, but rather as members of a class, trade, and family. And everyone, be he king or serf, was under the rule of God and bound in conscience by His laws; accepting in humility his state in life, most especially and unquestioningly his gender, and the duties imposed therein.

The rise of an independent merchant class from the eleventh to fourteenth century, the rebellion against the Church in the sixteenth century, and the philosophical dominance of individualism/liberalism in the seventeenth and eighteenth centuries caused a new Western society to come into being. The state became totally self-sufficient and all powerful, no longer constrained by a universal moral and spiritual arbitrator, deriving its power from those individuals who were enfranchised as full citizens—that is, men of wealth and property. Social classes and groupings remained, but no longer had an empowering group status since each man was looked upon as an individual, rather than as a member of a family, guild, or clan. The disenfranchised lower classes were at the complete mercy of the privileged body politic, who recognized no laws save their own.

This absolute and arbitrary power of the enfranchised elite became crushingly oppressive as it coalesced in the unbridled capitalism of the industrial revolution. As such, the disenfranchised were forced to seek political empowerment as a means of self-preservation. Two closely connected empowering movements that arose were Marxism and feminism; both sought liberation from patriarchal structures. But in the case of feminism it wasn't ideological liberalism in itself that caused the movement, but rather womanhood's loss of status; a status that had been derived from the indissoluble marriage bond. No longer pedestaled on the immovable and sacrosanct institution of marriage and family, women became socially vulnerable, subject to the caprices of both industrial capitalism and men's hearts. This loss of a woman's status in society—a status which included the opportunity to forgo marriage for the many facets of religious life—went hand in hand with the rejection of the authority of the Church; for it was the Protestant reformers that reduced marriage to a non-sacramental and dissolvable status and sought to eradicate the religious life.

The Proximate Causes

What began with the Protestant emancipation from the Church was to unavoidably culminate with the emancipation from God and His laws—including the intrinsic and elementary laws of gender. The final societal transformation was to begin after World War I, where emancipation was sought not only in the women's rights movement, but also in men's desire to adopt an extended adolescence or "playboy" lifestyle. Both trends sought freedom from prewar societal and familial structures and duties. Women sought freedom from the confines of the home and motherhood, men from the fatherly duties of providing, protecting, and leading.

In the United States, the Roaring Twenties commenced with the triumph of woman's suffrage (the nineteenth amendment, passed in 1920) and concluded with the social and the nearly wholesale religious acceptance of contraception (culminating with the Anglican Lambeth Council's acceptance in 1929). This postbellum decade of political rights and sexual license, witnessed women beginning to abandon the home in favor of a newly offered liberation. Canned foods, store bought clothes, and increased availability of transportation facilitated her flight-from domestic confines. The "flapper"[71] personified this new

---

71. "The term flapper in the 1920s referred to a 'new breed' of young women who wore short skirts, bobbed their hair, listened to the new jazz music, and flaunted

woman who sought liberation—not the least of which was sexual liberation—from the societal constraints of the prewar era. With the triumph of woman's suffrage in the early twenties, artificial contraception became the feminist's new banner issue. By the end of the decade contraception was given acceptance by all the major religious denominations save the Catholic Church.[72] In less than ten years, an act which had always been considered sinful was now considered virtuous and responsible by the West's moral guardians. For the next seventy years, similar 180 degree moral turnarounds would follow in rapid succession till the Western world's entire concept of right and wrong was itself turned topsy-turvy. The societal and moral upheaval that began in the twenties was to culminate in the final convulse of the sixties. Today's end result is a radically altered Western ethos and culture.

Men on their part initiated during the twenties the extended adolescence that has since so characterized the Western and American male. A playboy, a "boy at play," is a man who refuses to grow up, who lives merely for pleasure, fun, or entertainment. This new image of manhood enshrined adolescent values of self-gratification, such as sex, cars, sports, and parties. The coupling of these adolescent values with the social freedom and financial means of adulthood created the playboy. Feminism itself ascended with and was facilitated by this male mentality.

---

their disdain for what was then considered acceptable behavior. Flappers were seen as brash for wearing excessive makeup, drinking, treating sex in a casual manner, smoking, and otherwise flouting social and sexual norms." *Wikipedia: The Free Encyclopedia.* 22 Jun. 2008 <http://en.wikipedia.org/wiki/Flapper>.

72. In 1930 Pope Pius XI condemned contraception (and feminism) in his encyclical *Casti Connubii.* The Lambeth Council, the Anglican Church's synod of Bishops, one of the most respected and conservative ruling bodies in Protestantism, ruled officially in favor of allowing contraception, a little over a year before the issuance of Pius XI's encyclical, which many perceived to be evoked by that council's edict.

It wasn't the strident feminist ideologue that was instrumental in advancing the feminist agenda, rather it was the experience of women themselves who had had both their hearts and their homes broken by this new breed of undependable men that caused them to reject their role as the trusting, submissive wife. In fact, the liberated woman was the perfect mate for the new male; she was available without familial strings, leaving him free from the burdens of fatherhood or bonds of an ironclad marriage commitment.

It was in the twenties that entertainment and recreation were raised to such a level of importance that they began to dominate the conscience of the West by supplying both the culture's popular content and its identity. Frivolities were now pursued with the utmost seriousness. Recreational pursuits such as sports, games, dances, and the cinema supplied, for many, the meaning to life. Entertainment, with its power to propagandize, ruled the day, and subsequently the century. The exploits of movie stars and sports figures were frenziedly followed by an idolizing public. Yellow journalism and scandal sheets, whose objective was to entertain and whose subject matter was trite, became pervasive. A new Pantheon was erected and new celebrity gods enthroned, as the religion of secular humanism began its campaign of proselytism. The advent of the mass media facilitated accelerated the conversion of the West, especially the United States where it was most pervasive. As the mass entertainment media gained technical power, and a subsequent ubiquitous presence, it came to dominate the popular conscience and formulate the popular ethos: manipulating the values, ideals, beliefs, and self-image of a nation.

As the new postbellum ethos and a technically developing mass media gained ascendance, so did the first generation to grow up in its climate. Dubiously dubbed by some "the greatest generation," this generation's experience of the dull, gray poverty of the Great Depression only made the new ethos all that more enticing as it glimmered brighter still, and in color, on the silver screen. So too, the great effort this generation made during the Second World War only made the pursuit of peace and prosperity and the good life all that more desirable. In the U.S. it was this "greatest generation," which had experienced much privation and hardship, that would compromise all to be the first generation to realize the "American dream" *en masse*— presiding over the greatest increase in the standard of living mankind had ever experienced. The materialism and hedonism that were implicit in this generation's new ethos would become explicit and full blown in their children's (the baby-boomers) unrestrained pursuit of that same dream.

The society-wide adolescent rebellion of the sixties unconsciously challenged the integrity of a parental establishment that sought to maintain a semblance of traditional morals and a veneer of polite Christian behavior while their true motivational values stemmed from an ungodly materialism. It was under the watch of this first generation of the new ethos, at their apex of power, that the ideals of the twenties in which they were born were brought to a head and the remnant forces of the old order, an order nearly two thousand years old, were finally and soundly defeated. And it was this "greatest" generation whose patriarchy, losing control of the monster it had sired, weakly surrendered to a previously unimaginable, ever-metastasizing ethos; thus leaving the Western world, for the first time in its history, emasculated and fatherless.

The Current State of Affairs

In North America, as elsewhere, the vacuum of authority left by this final abdication of Western patriarchy has been eagerly filled by an expanding state. And today the secular state's power to control the lives and minds of its people is increased ten-thousand fold by technology. Technology facilitates the spread and effectiveness of bureaucracy, which is the state's infrastructure of power, management, and control. Bureaucratic structures in the past were limited in scope and power by the fact that after a certain point they became unwieldy and would collapse, but today, due to computerization and the internet, bureaucracy is able to stretch its tentacles across an entire nation and into each and every home. And technology, via the mass-media/ entertainment industry, has also allowed an unprecedented propagandizing of the masses to occur. This mesmerizing propaganda fills any gaps of thought or action not yet dictated by the state, as it systematically creates or destroys values and prepares the masses for the acceptance of state actions, such as the waging of foreign wars or domestic policing, or the creation of new-fangled rights which entails the rescinding of God-derived essential rights.

The Western rebellion against God-given authority symbolically began with the issue of divorce back in Henry VIII's time, and it has culminated with this same issue of divorce. What started with a king's legislation to reject the authority and sacred privilege of the Church now finds completion in the state's legislation to do away with the authority of fatherhood and sacred domain of the family. In the religious realm this rejection of divine authority destroyed Christian unity and the very fabric of Christendom. In the social realm it destroys the unity of the family and the very fabric of the body politic. (As such, it can be seen that St. Paul's teaching on the imaging of Christ's relationship of authority over His Church and a man's relationship of authority over his wife is no mere poetical relation but an intrinsic one, where the fortunes of one necessarily affect those of the other.)

The state, in granting itself the power to dissolve that which

God has joined, has given the evil of divorce the status of a right, which is liberal societies' highest moral good. In doing so, the state seems Hell bent on assuring that patriarchal, and hence familial, authority is stamped out completely. For divorce is not only a direct denial of the indissoluble, sacrosanct nature of marriage, but especially lethal to patriarchal authority. In the United States a growing number of states grant divorce automatically to the petitioner, no questions asked, reducing the marriage covenant to a status less binding than the simplest business contract. In the judicial eyes of the state a father has not a smidgen of authority over his family. In addition, the state, along with the politically correct mass media and all other secular organs of indoctrination and education (from grammar school to graduate school), continually encourage women to rebel. Hence, it is no accident that the vast majority of divorces are filed by women.[73]

As a follow up to the legislative and judicial destruction of the marriage vow, the state, as exemplified by the high-tech, bureaucratic government of the United States, has granted itself the right to actually intrude into the family home itself. It has done so with the creation of autonomous agencies that are purported to exist to prevent domestic violence and child abuse. Though these agencies are not subject to public election or approval, they have *carte blanche* power (requiring neither judicial nor legislative permission) to invade the home—even to take a child—on mere suspicion or allegation. In recent years the state and the mass media have launched powerful campaigns that, regardless of their claimed objective, result in the eradication of any last vestiges of parental and patriarchal authority and the sacrosanct status of the family. Examples of such campaigns include those whose rallying cries are "Stop

---

73. Divorce proceedings filed by women in the U.S. range from 72% to 88%.

Domestic Violence" and "Stop Child Abuse Before It Starts."
Both campaigns are accompanied by 800 numbers thus encouraging neighbors and friends to become informers for the state.
At face value, the first campaign's primary objective is to link
"domestic" and "violence" with one another. Domestic means
"having to do with the family," so, in fact, they are equating
violence with the family. The second campaign cited indicates
that even if you have not yet abused your child, according with
the state's construing of the word "abused," but show *indications*
that you might in the future, then the state can pre-emptively
intervene.

The best argument the state has in support of these campaigns is its statistics which indicate the epidemic proportions
of the problem. Yet these statistics are misleading at best. Not
only are social service agents not beyond inflating their figures
(a good bureaucrat perpetuates and expands the need for his
department), but the public isn't informed that nearly all of
these cases involve broken families, single mothers, fatherless
homes, and extra-marital affairs—in other words, they stem
from aberrations of the traditional family. In fact, statistics
show that it is in societies that are highly patriarchal, such as
those of a Hispanic makeup, that have the lowest incident of
assaults on wives, about half of that of the United States.

A closer scrutiny of the state's statistics shows that for
women the safest place is in a household with their lawful husbands; and for children, the safest place is in a household with
their biological fathers.

Children living in households with unrelated adults are
nearly fifty times as likely to die of inflicted injuries as children living with two biological parents, according to a study
of Missouri abuse reports published in the journal of the
American Academy of Pediatrics in 2005. Children living in
stepfamilies or with single parents are at higher risk of physical

or sexual assault than children living with two biological or adoptive parents, according to several studies co-authored by David Finkelhor, director of the University of New Hampshire's Crimes Against Children Research Center. Girls whose parents divorce are at significantly higher risk of sexual assault, whether they live with their mother or their father, according to research by Robin Wilson, a family law professor at Washington and Lee University.[74] Such being the case, the state should be trying to reinstate the traditional patriarchal family, if stemming domestic violence were its real agenda.

Of course society is duty bound to protect the innocent from violence. But it is the secular state itself and its ensuing society that accelerates the vicious circle of lawlessness, immorality, and violence. In a society that sanctions abortion, pornography, divorce, and the eradication of the traditional family, horrendous evils are bound to be unleashed. But heavy-handed state intervention only worsens the problem: As the family grows weaker in authority and virtue, so does the individual become less self-disciplined and virtuous; and it is left up to the state to reign in the mayhem. Hence the state intrudes itself into the familial and personal realms, which results in the further erosion of both familial and personal authority. And this perceived duty of the state to monitor and supplant familial authority effects not only dysfunctional families, but all families.

When the state takes upon itself the role of policing the home, then the home is no longer sacrosanct. And herein lies the problem: *the state does not weigh the good of the family against the good of the child.* It does not recognize that in its efforts to rectify an evil, it can perpetrate a greater evil. Such is the pitfall of any utopian ideology that seeks to create a perfect world, and it is

---

74. Donald G. Dutton, "Patriarchy and Wife Assault: The Ecological Fallacy," *Violence and Victims*, vol. 9, n. 2 (1994), pp. 167-182; as cited by Frank S. Zepezauer, "The Politics of Domestic Violence," The *Wanderer*, June 10, 1996.

made worse by the fact that the state seems unwilling to recognize that it is strong families that are the ultimate good for children, as well as wives and society as a whole. The state, then, does not discern an authentic hierarchy of goods, where the good and integrity of the family is to be sought first and foremost to best assure the good and well-being of its members. Due to this devaluation, the family, which was once afforded extra protection against governmental intrusion, now has less than ordinary protection against that intrusion. The modern state cannot brook any authority other than its own bureaucratic authority. And it is the family that "is the last bastion against tyranny," the last defense against an all-powerful state. Hence the state's great drive to usurp the God-given authority of the family and to incite familial rebellion; to unman fathers; and to lure women away from an exclusive devotion to the family. For the state, by means of its systemic disposition, intuits that if the family is united it will stand, but if divided— wife against husband, children against parents—it will fall or become nothing more than a mere sHell of its rightful self.

But, though all the powers of secular society—from the propagandizing of the mass media to social and economic re-engineering—are arrayed against familial and patriarchal authority, that authority must never cease to assert itself, for it is an authority that is God-given. For, as Pope Leo XIII so powerfully and succinctly put it: *"the father's power is of such a nature that it cannot be destroyed or absorbed by the state; for it has the same origin as human life itself."*[75] And therein lies the great battle of the twenty-first century, *a battle between state and family, bureaucracy and patriarchy, Christianity and secularism.* The powers of the state, augmented as they are by technology and by the propagandizing of the mass-media, have never been greater, nor as

---

75. Leo XIII, *Rerum Novarum.* Encyclical, 1891.

intrusive. Only an unbreachable family unity, one in Christ, will withstand this ungodly power, and it is only the Christian patriarchal hierarchy of the family that creates such a unity.

APPENDIX C

A Sample Mission Statement for a Proposed Boy's School of Christian Initiation

SAINT JOSEPH ACADEMY
"A School of Christian Initiation"

False and harmful to Christian education today is the so-called method of 'co-education' [which is founded] upon a deplorable confusion of ideas that mistakes a leveling promiscuity [i.e., an indiscriminate mixture of the sexes] and equality, for the legitimate association of the sexes. The Creator has ordained and disposed perfect union of the sexes only in matrimony, and, with varying degrees of contact, in the family and in society. Besides there is not in nature itself, which fashions the two quite different in organism, in temperament, and in abilities, anything to suggest that there can be or ought to be promiscuity, and much less equality, in the training of the two sexes. These in keeping with the wonderful designs of the Creator are destined to complement each other in the family and society, precisely because of their differences, which therefore ought to be maintained and encouraged during their years of formation, with the necessary distinction and corresponding separation, according to age and circumstances.

Pope Pius XI *Divini Illius Magistri*, Encyclical, 1929

Introduction

St. Joseph Academy is a school of Christian initiation dedicated to the development of tomorrow's Catholic leaders. As such, it seeks to convey to its young men the spiritual, moral, intellectual, and cultural constants of Catholicism in the context of secular society's overall intellectual accruement.

In addition to a rigorous course of studies, the process of Christian initiation entails the gradual inculcation of the character of Catholic manhood, the elemental mode in which all men manifest sanctity. In integral conjunction with the student's parents—specifically the father, who is the young man's primary and irreplaceable paradigm of manhood—the Academy seeks to graduate competent and zealous Catholic men: the fathers, the priests—*the saints*—of tomorrow.

St. Joseph Academy's program of studies is designed to convey essential knowledge, develop keen reasoning ability, and cultivate the beginnings of wisdom. The Academy ascribes to the pedagogy of the classical trivium, where the progressive actualization of intellectual potential is recognized and facilitated. This pedagogy finds correspondence in, and is enhanced by, the overall spiritual and moral formation objectives of the Academy. The courses in the humanities are especially integrated with each other and with this overall formation. Pertinent readings, selected from the humanities, are the focus of a weekly seminar. A college preparatory track in mathematics and science and various courses in the fine arts complete the curriculum.

The Academy's patron and patriarchal model is St. Joseph, the "just man" of the Gospels, and it is consecrated in its totality to the Blessed Virgin Mary under her title *Nuestra Senora de Guadalupe.*

Student Body

The Academy is intended for young men from the seventh grade to the twelfth grade who come from families ardently committed to living out the Catholic Faith with an ever-increasing integrity in thought and word, deed and lifestyle.

Principles of Education

All true knowledge and achievement is properly ordered towards knowing, loving, and serving the Lord: that is, the process of sanctification. It is in sanctification that one fulfills his personal potential. The Academy's end, therefore, is the facilitation of sanctity, the surest principle of academic and moral excellence.

An authentic Catholic curriculum recognizes objective truth as the unifying principle of all knowledge, and that all truth is authored by God. Hence, each subject of the Academy's curriculum is seen as a refraction of truth in varying modes and degrees and as having an intrinsic and objective relation to God. This theistic integration of the course of studies stresses the intrinsic value of each subject and the studious attention due it.

The study of Christian doctrine is the hub of the curriculum. For it is in comprehending the Faith—wherein resides the fullness of the truth—that the student best develops the concise reasoning ability to recognize and synthesize that which is true and recognize and refute that which is false, be the subject of a secular or theological nature.

Formal Function

A Christian school of initiation must be exhortative and prophetic, for it deals with the actualizing of human potential and with the future. At the same time its devotion to immutable truth, timeless and centered in Christ's advent, renders it necessarily traditional. It is the application of this truth in the context of the moment that imbues the school with its prophetic character. The formal nature of the teaching office facilitates this prophetic dynamic by allowing the school and its masters to uphold a standard that is exhortative: thus issuing a constant challenge to its student's spiritual, moral, and intellectual potential.

The Conveyance of Catholic Culture

Education in the fullest sense is the conveyance of culture: the sum of a tradition's accumulated knowledge, morals, and ways. The Academy seeks to achieve this fullness of education. A Catholic culture is one that manifests the truths, values, and beliefs of the Faith and excludes those that are contrary to it. It is a given that, especially in today's milieu, such a culture is counter to that of the world's. As such, students are expected to manifest the Faith with a courageous militancy.

Catholic culture ensues to the degree that the Faith is fully integrated into daily life. The Academy, enabled by its formal character, will attempt to facilitate this process by setting challenging standards within its domain.

The Call to Christian Manhood

Fathers are expected to be their sons' main mentor during their attendance at the Academy. While understanding that his son is still in the process of becoming a man, the father must, nonetheless, expect him, in no uncertain terms, to embrace and strive for, both intellectually and morally, the ideals of manhood, and in so doing form the foundation for the lifelong process of perfecting one's manhood. Academy masters are to work in conjunction with the student's fathers in this pursuit.

Fathers are to be the primary parental contact with the

Academy. (See *Academy Organization and Faculty Forum* below).
Paternal sponsors will be required for those young men who
are without the presence of their fathers.

Principles of Moral Formation

Moral formation, which entails character development and will
training, is an integral part of an authentic Catholic education.
Academy students are required to make continued progress
in scholarly discipline and Catholic virtue as indicative of an
overall pursuit of sanctity. Such progress is measured by the
following criteria (these principles are partially based on those
found in a "General Statement of Philosophy of the American
Jesuit High School," *Jesuit Educational Quarterly,* October 1946):

1) Persevering application to study and progressive mastery
   of the academic subject matter.
2) Submission to intellectual and moral discipline.
3) Cultivation of scholarly humility that corresponds with
   academic achievement.
4) Pursuing studies and participating in the Academy day
   with a
   cheerful disposition and a spirit of respect and grati-
   tude for the educational opportunity provided by the
   Academy and the parents.
5) A life of self-discipline that is motivated by Catholic
   moral and supernatural principles of conduct rather
   than by impulses from within or circumstances from
   without.

In order to achieve these ends parents must be supportive
of, and work with, the Academy as it prescribes disciplinary or
academic remedies on behalf of their son.

Christian Initiation and Self-Discipline

The discipline of Christian initiation is not specifically characterized by imposed discipline but rather by the fostering of self-discipline. In order for the young man to mature morally and spiritually he must begin to internalize and make his own the values and ideals of both the Faith and his family.

Those in charge of his formation, the father foremost, must adopt an attitude that views the youth as an apprentice and initiate to manhood. The key pedagogical principle of a school of Christian initiation is to treat the student like a man and expect him to act as such. If the student fails to live up to this expectation he is subsequently deprived of, to a degree proportional to his offense, the honor of being treated like a man. But punishment is necessarily coercive and does not directly entail the principle of self-discipline. Punishment, therefore, is to be used always within the overall context of promoting the goal of self-discipline and not as a primary means of adolescent formation; and it need not be if the young man received adequate coercive discipline in his childhood.

Student Comportment

Students are expected to comport themselves in accord with justice and Christian honor by rendering that which is due to Christ, Church, Family, and Academy (see appendix C). The just man is truthful, obedient, liberal, pious, and religious. During the school day these traits will be made manifest in the student's religious reverence, amiable and respectful attitude toward Academy faculty, and his graceful acceptance of academic rigors. Specifically the student is expected to exhibit a cheerful, grateful, and humble attitude while at the Academy. Students are also expected to self-regulate their private conversations in accord with the above traits of justice. Disparaging remarks concerning faculty members, parents, or members of the hierarchy are to be regarded as infractions against piety.

In addition, the Academy hopes that Christian charity (that which goes beyond honor, beyond that which is strictly due) will manifest itself in the lives of its students. It is desired, therefore, that the Academy student body views itself as a Christian brotherhood, and renders fraternal respect accordingly.

Disciplinary Actions

Belligerence towards Academy authorities, premeditated cheating (e.g., use of "crib notes"), or grave violations of the Commandments or Church teachings, will warrant immediate suspension. Chronic minor violations that show little improvement will also eventually result in suspension. At the end of the suspension period a meeting with the parents and student will be held to consider re-admittance.

Repetitive calisthenics, writing assignments, and after-school work orders will be imposed for lesser offenses.

Study requirements

Homework will be given daily. In addition to homework assignments, the student is expected to study: that is, review the past day's lessons and preview the next day's lessons. Parental monitoring of their son's homework and study progress is essential. Since class preparation takes place in the home the instilling of study habits is the parent's responsibility.

Students are expected to view each subject of the curriculum as a partial manifestation of God's truth, and therefore diligently and cheerfully apply themselves to its study.

Academic and Home Environment

The Academy maintains a cloistered environment that seeks to lessen the secular influences of the world, while fostering individual sanctity and the development of a distinctly Catholic culture. Such an environment will be both prayerful and scholarly.

So too, a home environment that is non-contradictory to that of the Academy is expected. Integral to such an environment is a valid marital union as defined by the Code of Canon Law of the Catholic Church. In addition, a certain barring of the secular (inclusive of the "pop culture" of the mass media) and nurturing of the sacred is urged.

Academy Organization and Faculty Forum

The Academy faculty includes all staff, teachers, and fathers (or designated male proxy) of students. Periodic faculty meetings will be scheduled to work on Academy business, to study and discuss pertinent theological, moral, or political issues (especially those that deal with the dynamics of Catholic manhood), and to engage in devotional exercises. All faculty members are expected to attend the meetings.

Faculty members will attempt to reach unanimity on issues (not covered by policy) that are controverted, such as those of a historical or political nature. These issues will be discussed in an attempt to reach a Catholic conclusion: that is, one that is moral and demonstrative of Christian charity. Political orientation will not be a factor.

While faculty members are encouraged to assist the director in his duties, in accord with the principles of hierarchical government full authority for all Academy philosophy, policy, and practical matters remains entirely his.

Family Interview

A formal interview with the director of the Academy is required of all families, inclusive of the prospective student, seeking enrollment. Families will be notified by letter, telephone, or e-mail of the admission interview's outcome.

Logistics

The academic schedule will be determined in accord with the number of students, their grade span, and the economic use of faculty members. Initially, grade levels can be expected to be combined into sections (e.g., 7-8, 9-10).

Practice of the Faith

If possible, daily Mass (mandatory for all students) will be offered at the Academy; if not, the daily commencement of classes will allow students time to attend Mass at their parishes.

The Academy seeks to maintain a traditional observance of the Faith: liturgically, devotionally, and culturally.

The Academy's standards and content are guided by the teachings of the Holy Catholic Church, and its staff and faculty submit themselves in obedience to her Magisterium.

Development and Documentation of Academy Philosophy and Policy

The Academy will continually seek to perfect its formal adherence to, and exhortation of, the Catholic Faith and culture, and to improve its curriculum. As such, Academy documentation of philosophy and policy can be expected to undergo refinement of definition. As a refinement such definition will be harmonious with previous editions. Full documentation (inclusive of this philosophy pamphlet, a student handbook, and a faculty/parent handbook) of Academy philosophy and policy will be provided. Modifications in curriculum, scheduling, or other practical matters will be presented, if at all possible, well in advance of the academic year in which they are to be implemented.